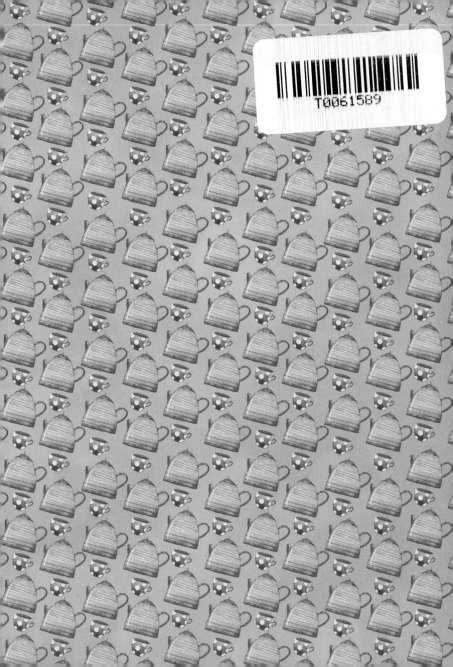

T0061589

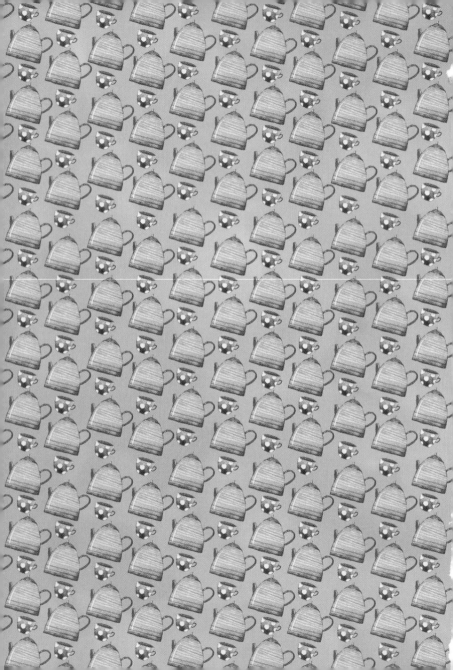

A Tea Witch's Grimoire

A TEA WITCH'S GRIMOIRE

Magickal Recipes for Your Tea Time

S. M. HARLOW

WEISER BOOKS

This edition first published in 2023 by Weiser Books, an imprint of
Red Wheel/Weiser, LLC
With offices at:
65 Parker Street, Suite 7
Newburyport, MA 01950
www.redwheelweiser.com

ISBN: 978-1-57863-821-5

Library of Congress Control Number: 2023930510

Cover and text design by Sky Peck Design
Interior illustrations copyright © S_Artlove, Talloshau Illustrations,
Bridgett Stahlman Design, A_Ptichkina via Creative Market

Typeset in Footlight
Printed in China
LPP
10 9 8 7 6 5 4 3 2

This is for you, Abuelita.

Contents

The Tea Witch

A sweet pea-covered cottage nestled in a vast and colorful garden . . . a single soul gathering herbs by the light of the moonflowers . . . a copper teapot hissing and bubbling with ancient magick. Walk up the cobblestone path edged with red creeping thyme and ring the bell. The tea witch always welcomes you to sit by the hearth and share the secrets of her craft.

A *Tea Witch's Grimoire* holds the carefully crafted tea recipes that might be found within any witch's old dusty cupboard. Herbal teas, elixirs, potions waiting for those who come to seek their heart's desire: love, healing, protection, fertility, wealth, beauty, and more.

This humble guide will deliver treasures of a long-kept practice that has not often been brought to the light. Begin with magickal recipes that fulfill the ordinary needs of everyday life. Then continue on to explore tea rituals that will tantalize and delight. Explore potions that can bring even the most hardened hearts to their unchanging truths.

Ring the bell to this little cottage and explore the warm magick of this tea witch's endless cup of lore.

Simple Pleasures and Magick

This grimoire, or "spell book," contains sacred recipes that this tea witch holds true and dear. In the daily practice of the magickal arts, the spirit desires enlightenment but also seeks nourishment and comfort. By our hands, we create earthly substances of vast power, and by our hearts, we tend to the fires of our soul.

Such herb brews, potions, spells, and magick act well to please and serve. Yet one must remember that they are but an extension of one's power to be incorporated into the larger acts of the imagination and the arcane arts. The Great Wisdom that may be sought within these pages is the source that transforms a simple hand gesture into a powerful magickal tool in a simple teacup. It is the greatest of virtues to see the larger realm of magick within the homeliest of recipes.

And thus, we witness that the spirit's wisdom is manifested within the artful use of tea magick.

I will always remember the inviting smells and the warmth and love of my grandmother's kitchen. I would so often find her creating some odd yet delicious remedies and explaining to me—even though I was a young child—what these concoctions could do and how their power was helped along with love and faith. My grandmother was a healer. The moment she would see you, she seemed to know right away what was needed. Strangers flocked to her, old friends never strayed far, and the large family she was blessed to raise knew her to be a mother who sacrificed so much for the happiness of others.

How she devoted herself to healing the *familia* in every kind of way. She inspired me. Inspired many. And she made me wish to become a healer like herself and tap into that intuition that seemed to never fail her in bringing peace among family, soothing mental distress, and finding love when it was needed.

I am still growing and journeying the tea magick path. I am not yet the tea witch my grandmother was—she was a true Wise Woman from years of her own journey. But her memory lives on in the recipes I make, the remedies I give, and in the faith and love I inspire to gift to the world. She taught me that if the heart is humble in everything you do, and you stay connected to the energies that be, you can be the healer that is needed. Through her teachings and the wisdom I have gained on my own life journey, tea witchery has found a place in my craft that has felt more like the warm and comforting walls of my grandmother's kitchen than any other practice.

So, join me in this tea witchery world. May it bring you the same healing and magick that my dear grandmother's spirit brought me.

Beginning the Craft

his book—this tea witch's grimoire—will share with you ancestral recipes for creating herbal tea blends for many different magickal purposes. I also include a special section on how to empower your teas: through the use of crystals, sigils, and with a variety of potions recipes—all of which can be added to your teas to enhance specific and powerful magickal properties. You will also find an appendix of elemental qualities of herbs, and a handy list of herb substitutions if any of the botanicals herein are not available to you, whether due to location or season. Finally, you'll learn what to do with your herbs once the tea has been prepared and used and gone—this is a powerful magickal step in tea witchery that is often overlooked in other tea grimoires. At the end of your tea ritual or spell, you can use the leaves for divination, and—importantly—you will learn how to dispose of what remains in a responsible (and powerfully magickal) way.

What Is Tea?

What most people commonly think of as "tea" are usually black teas, green teas, oolongs, dark teas (such as pu-erh tea)—there are even white teas and yellow teas. What all these teas have in common is they are brews made from variants of the plant *Camellia sinensis*—the tea plant. This grimoire will contain plenty of recipes that include this botanical, but the tea witch draws on the magick of many botanicals—the vast sources of power offered to use through the earth. Any reference to "tea" in this grimoire will refer to all

sorts of botanical brews. The recipe ingredients herein will create your "tea blend"; and infusing or steeping that blend in water will create the drink, which will just be referred to as the "tea." All of the recipes in this book will create a single cup of tea, unless specifically noted otherwise. Any tea brew can be prepared for more than one individual—just increase the ingredients in the tea brew proportionally.

Preparing Your Herbs

When beginning the craft, you'll first need some basics of how to gather, prepare, and store your herbs and flowers.

HERB DRYING AND STORAGE

Herbs can be dried in the oven, or dehydrator, or hanged. Herbs may also be frozen and stored for later uses. The best times to harvest your herbs are either in the morning, after the dew has dried on the leaves or in the early evening. The best stage to harvest herbs is just before they flower; this is when you can find the best flavor. If you decide to ever gather seeds, such as for fennel, dill, or caraway, you can see the seeds forming as the heads fade out. Pick the stalks just as they start to turn brown and hang them upside down in a tied brown paper bag. The seeds will fall into the bag.

OVEN DRYING

Set your oven at the lowest temperature. Arrange your herbs on a single layer on a wire rack lined with cheesecloth. Place in the oven and leave the door slightly ajar. Turn the herbs every half hour until they are dry and crumbly.

DEHYDRATOR DRYING

Place the herbs in a single layer on an herb screen in the dehydrator. Leave in the dehydrator until the leaves are dry and brittle. Rotate the trays if necessary.

AIR DRYING

Cut sprigs several inches in length, then strip the bottom to expose a few inches of stem. Gather small bundles of your herbs, but remember to keep them loose; you will want them to be able to breathe through the drying process. Tie them together, just tight enough that they won't

come apart when they shrink from drying. Use cotton string. Hang the bunch upside down in a warm, dry place, out of direct sunlight. It takes approximately two weeks for the herbs to dry, depending upon the humidity of your area. They should be completely brittle and crumbly. Air drying is often the best practice, as it helps keep the color, flavor, and magick contained in the herbs. The ideal temperature for air drying is 100 degrees, but in cooler temperatures, it will simply just take the herbs longer to dry. If you are trying to dry herbs that are too small to bundle, you may also place them on screens to air dry. But be sure to rotate and turn the leaves every other day to ensure they dry completely.

STORING DRIED HERBS

When dried, remove any stems, roots, or thorns and place in an airtight container. Store in a cool, dark, dry place for up to one year. For specific enchanted herbs, you may place symbols on the container to add power to their energy.

If you choose to freeze your fresh herbs instead, then this will help ensure to preserve their fresh flavor and energy. Chop the herbs and place one teaspoon into each cube of an ice cube tray, then spoon one teaspoon of water over the herbs and freeze. Store the cubes in an airtight container in the freezer. Take out as many cubes as needed. You may also choose to vacuum seal your herbs and place in an airtight container in a cellar or in the freezer.

Magickal Tea Tools

Tea witchery, similar to many ceremonial rituals among different practices of the Craft, has its own tools for use in spells and rituals. These tools carry their own elements, energies, and magickal correspondences.

It is lovely to build a tea altar with your own consecrated tools when the perfect opportunity comes up to cast a remedy or a quick ritual. Or simply become aware of the magick your tea tools contribute and offer to extend your own hand of power to the herbs. The most ideal and powerful tea tools are family tokens, passed down from generation to generation. Older tools carry the most power. But this is not necessary and not always possible. Any tea witch may begin from the start and build their own cupboard of magickal delights, filled with items that sing their personality, vibrate with their love, and are infused by the brewer's essence, thus giving their tea tools the magick to distribute any remedy.

While tools in the craft have often been taught to hold energies traditionally referred to as either "masculine" or "feminine," when it comes to magickal correspondences, do not think of these as connected to or reflective of gender or sexual orientation. These terms are simply to denote energetic quality so that you may balance energies within a space while you are using the tool.

KNIFE/HERB SCISSORS

A tool for the element of fire. Carries masculine energies. Often a white handle is best. May be placed in the south end of the tea tray. Helps to direct energy within the space. Great for cutting away negative

energies, summoning protection, and charging and consecrating herbs.

TEASPOON/SPOONS

A tool for the element of air. Carries masculine energies. A tool of invocation because it serves as the will of the brewer and summons their energy to the forefront. Used to charge the brew, bestow blessings, draw down energies during ritual, and evoke the spirits–deities–or ancestors. May be placed on the east end of your tea tray. Spoons may be made of wood, metals, heatproof glass, and sometimes water and heatproof safe gemstones.

TRIVET/TEA WARMER

A tool for the element of earth. Carries feminine energies.

A grounding tool to calm and balance the energies of the ritual space. Aids in protecting the space. May be placed in the north end of the tea tray. Trivets or tea warmers are typically made of cast iron, ceramic, or glass.

TEAPOT/TEACUP/KETTLE

A tool for the element of water. Carries feminine energies. Symbolizes the containment and the womb of the goddess or sacred energies. To bless the sacred waters, brews, and libations for rituals and

spells. It is symbolic of inspiration, rebirth, illumination, abundance, manifestation, and rejuvenation, thus making it the ultimate tool for general conjuring. For not only does it represent the element of water, but also the element of spirit. Brings that which is not yet reality into our physical realm.

TEA TRAY

Tool encompassing all the elements. Carries both masculine and feminine energies. The tea tray creates a space that essentially is the circle of your ritual, uniting all the energies of each magickal tool. Summons a protective boundary and balances the energies. Tea trays may be made from wood, metals, or even gemstones, and carved or painted with sacred symbols.

Tea Remedies

ere we begin with the methods and means for certain magick that may be acquired to benefit both the body and the mind. When practiced daily, these rites will elevate your nature and bring about your envisioned needs, for these are not only remedies but also spells to manifest. Study and remember these practices and the herbs that benefit your desire, and gift yourself greater ease and clarity by performing these spells and rituals.

If you can, it is good to work with fresh herbs from the garden or foraged in the wild while they still have all their strength. Hang them where they can dry, if possible warmed by the hearth. This will guarantee their power will be preserved. When the time is right, and desire calls, bring together the rightful herbs in your most favored teapot of good size. Create the space. Be mindful as you fill the kettle with fresh boiling water and allow the tea to steep. Pour it out into a faithful cup and drink the infusion while it is hot. And never forget the intentions behind every moment. Never stress if you are without a strong cast-iron pot, glass kettle, or anything else these spells require. Let the magick become your own. These remedies are only but a guide. The true magick resides within you.

Though simple it may sound,
this is where the wisdom can truly be found.
For it is when you honor the tea as it deserves,
a faithful friend it becomes and serves.

Happiness Tea

To fill the heart and space with needed happiness, obtain a large, wide white mug with beautiful, illustrated flowers. Blend your recipe within this large vessel. Take your honey and begin to drizzle over the herbs a heart shape sigil. Hover your hands over the mug and invoke energies of joy, optimism, and peace of mind from your guiding spirits. Breathe over your mix to give the tea its spark of life. Boil your water and steep this tea for 4 to 6 minutes. Strain. Prepare lemon slices and add to your tea. Let the lemon serve as an added charm to enhance your heart's acceptance for happiness.

1 teaspoon red clover
1 teaspoon lavender
¼ teaspoon marjoram
1 teaspoon honey

Especially favored when shared with others between the new waxing moon and the full moon.

Peace Tea

To be served to others in the home when tempers are high, this tea is especially good for quarreling couples to ease their anger and to inspire forgiveness. You must match the number of fresh sprigs of thyme to the number of people who need peace (for example, two angry people, two sprigs of thyme). The thyme will serve as their poppets. Bring the sprigs together and bind with cooking twine. As you do so, focus your intent on whom these branches represent and how they may make peace with one another. Place these in a blue or white teapot. Gently shower the other ingredients over the shoots. Know that passionflower will bring communication, calm, and honesty, and that the violet blossoms will soothe their wounds and protect the heart from the pain getting worse. Slowly bring a pot to boil; no need to rush. Brew the tea for 5 to 7 minutes. If possible, encourage people to sweeten each other's tea, or to pass the honey around.

1 teaspoon passionflower
1 teaspoon violet blossoms
2 to 3 sprigs fresh thyme
1 teaspoon honey

This tea may also be drunk alone to simply instill peace throughout your being.

A Loving Tea Bath Spell

Bring a pot of water to a boil. While waiting, blend this recipe within a clear bowl. Lovingly focus your energy and caress your hands through the herbs to further empower the blend. Once well blended, breathe over your mix to give the tea its spark of life. Add a tablespoon to a tea strainer within a pink or white mug. Steep for 5 to 6 minutes. Sweeten.

1 teaspoon rose petals
1 teaspoon hibiscus
1 teaspoon yarrow
1 tablespoon dried strawberries
1 teaspoon sugar

Prepare a bath and set around it numerous rose quartz, pink, or white lit candles. Bring about and steep within its depths your favorite scented strawberry or rose bath salts. Bare yourself freely and enter the hot bath. Sit within the bath, clutching the cup of tea against your heart.

Chant seven times:

> *I am love and my perception of love is divine.*
> *I embody this love for I am my own shrine.*

At the end of each chant, drink this tea. Once complete, proceed to bathe yourself with love with rose- or strawberry-scented soap. Caress your skin, heart, and face with rose quartz. This spell is either to attract love to you, to heal the heart, or to strengthen self-love. The tea recipe may also be served to others to inspire love either within themselves or toward the brewer. Couples may drink to strengthen the love between them. Great tea for weddings. Best done on Fridays during the waxing moon.

Luck Tea Sachet

To manifest luck toward any situation at hand, especially when having to do with business or money matters. Best when done at the start of the waxing moon.

You will need:

2 orange candles
1 fine large muslin bag
A large white teacup
A citrine stone

Set the white teacup between the two burning orange candles. Place the citrine stone inside your muslin bag. Keep nearby.

Blend the following together inside the white teacup:

4 tablespoons linden flowers
4 dashes ground allspice
4 dashes ground nutmeg
4 dashes ground cinnamon
4 tablespoons dried orange peel
4 tablespoons black tea
4 star anises

Blend in that order, where the star anise will be the last ingredient on top. Hover your hands over the herbal blend.

Chant:

> *The star is the guiding light,*
> *I desire luck with all my might.*
> *By the power of these spices and tea,*
> *Luck will find me.*

Fill the fine muslin bag with your tea blend. Use 1 teaspoon of this tea in your cup, making sure to include one star anise, and enjoy as the candles burn down. You may add a splash of hazelnut milk and honey. Keep the tea blend with you everywhere you go and brew a cup every day for four days. After steeping, remove herbs, but be sure to always leave a star anise within your cup until you are done.

Purification Tea

Drink before rituals or spells to cleanse the energies within and around you. Prepare a large glass bowl filled with sea salt and clear quartz the night before. Place a small glass plate over it, and on the plate blend together your recipe. Allow the tea blend to rest and charge overnight. When ready, boil a pot of water in a glass kettle. Steep the tea in a glass mug for 7 to 10 minutes. Strain and enjoy.

1 teaspoon vervain
1 teaspoon lemon verbena
1 tablespoon dried lemon peel
1 sprig fresh rosemary
1 teaspoon coconut sugar

May also be served to a friend in need of purification with a splash of coconut milk.

Health Tea Sachet Spell

Place the following ingredients in a circle. In the center, place an earthen bowl. You will need to possess or sew together a large green sachet with golden ribbon or yarn. To one side of the bowl, place a lit gold or yellow candle. To the other side of the bowl set a censer that is burning rosemary incense. Before blending your recipe, wave your hands above the golden flame, then through the smoke of rosemary incense. Proceed to blend the tea within the earthen bowl, using your hands and your breath. Focus on the full intent for stabilized health.

1 tablespoon rose-scented geranium

1 tablespoon mint

2-4 sprigs fresh marjoram

2-4 sprigs fresh thyme

Once done, scoop the tea blend into the sachet and tie it three times around with one piece of string. Pass the sachet through the incense then over the candle's flame, then hold it within your palms.

Chant three times:

The Earth is a giving mother;
our health she nurtures and harbors.

Keep the sachet within an earthen container and brew when you need to maintain good health and spirits. This tea will also help keep worries and anxieties at bay. Best done on a Sunday, or during a new moon.

Divination Tea Ritual

This is a wonderful recipe to drink before or during divination work. A pinch of mugwort may be added to enhance the senses, especially if done before bed.

Prepare a space with a purple cloth, or a cloth that has been used for divination. Choose either purple, black, or white candles to burn around the space. Place clear quartz, obsidians, or moonstones around the cloth. Choose your preferred divination tool and set this at the center of the cloth. Beside it, place a clear glass mug.

As you bring water to a boil in a clear glass kettle, place a glass bowl over a mirror plate. Blend your recipe in this bowl and focus your intentions. Give it your breath of life. Prepare yourself a brewed cup using a tablespoon of the blend. Steep for 8 to 10 minutes. Sweeten with honey, if desired.

1 tablespoon dandelion root
1 tablespoon hibiscus
1 tablespoon dried orange peel
1 tablespoon dried fig

Use this same tea blend to sprinkle a circle around your divination tools and teacup.

Chant as you do this:

Oracles of divine light,
Send me my second sight.
Bless the tools that make it so,
Bring the visions for me to know.

Longevity Tea Ritual

Drink when honoring life itself. Promotes a long individual life, blessed with health and wisdom. A perfect tea to brew during the spring and summer rites. Choose one or more of the following flowers for your ceremony:

carnations • chrysanthemums • lavender
lilies • orchids • roses • sunflowers

Cover a table with a white, blue, or green cloth. Place a glass or silver tray in the center with a floral teapot. Arrange the flowers around this tray along with a handful of white, blue, or green candles. In a decorative floral bowl, blend the recipe. Breathe over the tea to give it that spark of life energy.

1 tablespoon dried apple pieces
1 teaspoon rose hips
1 tablespoon dried lemon peel
1 teaspoon lavender
1 teaspoon sage

Brew this tea loosely within the teapot for 5 to 7 minutes and light your candles. Touch the flowers and deeply breathe their fresh scent. You may also play sound bowls or other meditative music during the ceremony. Raise your cup to the heavens.

Chant:

Goddess of mercy, loving and kind,
Grant us the serenity of a long life.

Binding Tea Spell

When you have need to bind yourself from a bad habit or to bind someone else from doing harm to themselves or to others, brew this faithful tea spell.

You will need:

A black mug
Strong black tea bag with string attached
A black felt-tip marker
Splash of hazelnut milk

Create a symbol that represents what needs to be bound. It can be an image or a word (but consider an image if you are serving this to another). Draw or write this image or word on the tag of the tea that hangs out of the cup. Then, as you are focusing on what needs to be bound, begin to tie nine knots from the tag, down the string, to the tea bag.

Chant aloud after each knot is tied:

With each knot, my will be done.

Brew the tea and serve with a splash of hazelnut milk, but no sugar or honey! When disposing of the tea bag, collect and wrap the string tightly around the bag, seal it in a jar, and hide it in a dark place where it will never be disturbed.

Prophetic Sleep Tea

This tea is best blended when a full moon is at its peak. In a clear glass bowl, blend the following tea ingredients and place an amethyst tower at its center.

1 teaspoon elder flowers

1 teaspoon passionflower

1 teaspoon thyme

1 teaspoon valerian root

1 teaspoon rosebuds

Bring your dish outdoors, raise it between your hands, above your head, and to the night sky. Be sure the tea and crystal are flooded with moonlight.

Chant:

Sweet Grandmother Moon,
Giver of sight,
Bless this tea,
To bring me visions tonight.

Boil a pot of water and steep this tea for 8 minutes. You may add honey and coconut milk to sweeten the visions. Enjoy your tea before bed. Repeat the chant, all the while focusing on the kind of visions you are seeking to have. Place the amethyst tower under your pillow to sleep upon. Be sure to have a dream journal to write down your dreams when you awake.

Psychic Protection Tea

You will need:

A black cup with a saucer
Black salt
Spoon
Strainer
1 teaspoon lavender
1 teaspoon lemon balm
1 teaspoon peppermint
1 sprig fresh rosemary

Begin this spell remedy by envisioning the cup as yourself, and the saucer as your world and your surroundings. Blend the tea within the cup, focusing on its powers to cleanse and protect you from all that is icky within. Then take your black salt and sprinkle it counterclockwise around the outside of your cup on the saucer. Focus on the black salt's powers to banish and protect you from anything around you that is trying to attack psychically. Have a pot of hot water ready and brew for 6 to 9 minutes. As it is steeping, lean forward and breathe in the hot aroma, allowing the spell to enter in and replenish your senses and boost your protection. Strain, add a splash of coconut milk and a teaspoon of honey. Stir counterclockwise. Drink knowing you are now protected from any psychic attacks. Best when done between the new and waning moons.

Tarot Tea

You will need:

A deck of tarot cards
An amethyst
A purple mug with strainer
1 teaspoon black tea
1 tablespoon dried cherries
1 teaspoon peppermint
1 vanilla bean

When you have time to yourself and you can sit in peace and quiet, bring a pot to boil. Blend your tea within your strainer and use a whole vanilla bean by slicing halfway down its stem. With the amethyst in your left hand, hover your right hand over the herbs. Infuse your energy and intentions into them, using the crystal to amplify your gifts as a seer. Then breathe your spark of life into the recipe. Pour the hot water over your tea and steep for 3 minutes. As it is brewing, make yourself comfortable and clear your mind. Breathe deeply and get into a meditative state. Strain and sweeten your tea, if desired. Use the vanilla bean to stir clockwise. Take your time and savor your brew deeply. Once ready, shuffle your tarot deck three times, all the while visualizing yourself walking down a long hallway. Picture yourself approaching a door. Upon this door, knock three times, simultaneously knocking on your tarot deck as well. Envision the door opening and call out to your spirit guides. Cut the deck into three piles with your dominant hand.

- The first pile is a symbol of the past.

- The second pile is a symbol of the present, and events currently unveiling.

- The third pile is a symbol of the future.

Using your dominant hand, select the card on top of each pile. Focus on each card and examine the way each one makes you feel. Observe the symbols and the sensations you receive. Absorb this information and allow your other psychic senses to align and come through. Call out to your guides and ask for the cards to be explained to you. Take as long as you need. When you and the cards have connected and you have received your answers, write down your reading.

To Ward Off Negativity

Bring a small cast-iron pot of water to a slow gentle boil. As it is heating, blend the following recipe in a black dish or a mini cauldron.

1 tablespoon black tea
1 cinnamon stick
½ teaspoon hyssop
1 slice lemon
1 sprig fresh rosemary

Sift the blend with your left fingers, all the while focusing your intentions on dispelling negative energies from within or around you. Loudly huff your breath of life into the herbs. Once the water is boiled, take it off the heat and let sit for 3 minutes. Drop your herbs into the pot; let steep for another 3 minutes. While the tea is brewing, light a cinnamon stick to create an incense. Waft the smoke counterclockwise over the brew, while chanting:

Smoke and fire burning bright,
Turn my darkness into light.
Water and earth brewing true,
Dispel the negativity and leave anew.

Place the burning cinnamon stick nearby where you will be drinking your remedy. Place a strainer over your mini cauldron. With a ladle, pour your brew into the cauldron. If you wish to sweeten with honey, use the fresh rosemary to stir in counterclockwise. Drink and visualize the negativity washing away within and around you.

Prosperity Tea Ritual

Set up an altar with green altar cloth, red candles, green aventurine, carnelian, garnet, and jade stones. Choose decor that fits the occasion. Begin bringing a pot of new-moon water to a boil. Place a wooden bowl at the center of your altar and blend together the recipe with a wooden spoon. Stir clockwise while using your breath to spark life into your tea. Empower the blend with your thoughts of prosperity and luck.

> 1 teaspoon mullein
> 1 teaspoon vetiver
> 1 teaspoon mint
> 1 teaspoon lemon balm
> 2 teaspoons honey

Brew the tea for 5 to 7 minutes. Sweeten with 2 tsp honey. Sit and meditate at your altar. Burn any luck-drawing incense, or you may even burn the same recipe above over charcoal. Feel the flow of all that is light and good enter your being. Breathe in this energy and release it in the space around you. On the last inhaled breath, sip the tea to seal the light within.

Chant seven times:

> *As the flow of luck be everlasting,*
> *may my luck be ever lifting.*

Drink when you need prosperity, luck, money, and/or success. This tea invites all aspects into the brewer's life. Best done on a Thursday, or during a new moon.

Astral Travel Tea

Place a glass bowl between four clear quartz towers. Blend together your recipe using a glass spoon or a glass stirring stick. Leave the tea to rest between the crystals to absorb and channel their energy for several hours. In a heat-safe glass kettle, bring to a boil purified water that has previously been left out under the full moonlight. Scoop 2 to 3 tablespoons of the tea blend into a clear glass pot, add boiled water, and let brew for about 10 to 15 minutes.

1 tablespoon spearmint
½ teaspoon mugwort
½ teaspoon angelica root
1 star anise

Sit in a safe, comfortable space. Choose to enjoy the silence or have a playlist of drums or sound bowls playing in the background. Burn an incense of mugwort or sandalwood, or a blend of both. Get comfortable and focus your gaze deep into the depths of your brew.

Chant over the tea three times:

The door is open, and I shall take flight.
My spirit will soar to new grander heights.

As you sip on the tea, allow yourself to slip into a trancelike state to break free from your body and step forward into the other realms. Or follow the path within and strengthen your psychic visions and mental powers. For additional power, add a dash of ginger. Best done on a Monday, or during a waxing moon.

Aura Repair Tea

When you feel drained, moody, tired, or lifeless, it may be time to cleanse and align the aura and chakras. This tea spell may become a regular part of your beauty routine, such as for a weekly spa day.

Prepare the bathroom. Cover the counters and bathtub with quartz, Himalayan pink salt lamps, seashells, and pink and/or white candles. Prepare the recipe either in a clear glass bowl or in a large abalone shell. Bless and enchant your blend with your breath of life.

> 1 teaspoon peppermint
> 1 teaspoon hibiscus
> ¼ teaspoon lemongrass
> ⅛ teaspoon mugwort
> 1 sprig fresh rosemary
> 1 teaspoon coconut sugar

You can choose to either brew this tea for 5 to 10 minutes to drink, or place the tea blend into a cheesecloth sachet and brew it into the bathwater itself. Proceed with your purifying beauty routine, such as a facial, hair treatment, and a long deep soak in the bath.

To Break a Love Spell Tea

Prepare the table that the tea will be served on. There must be two candleholders at the center of a white table runner. You will need two black candles and a needle for carving. Beneath each candle, carve the initials of the one whom the spell is cast upon and the one who is casting it. If it is unknown who the caster is, then the initials of the one who is spelled may be carved into both. Use candle glue to secure the candles into the holders. These candles must be lit the moment the person(s) enter the space.

Blend together on a cast-iron plate:

1 teaspoon blue vervain
1 teaspoon hawthorn berries
1 teaspoon rose hips
pistachio milk to serve

Brew a strong pot of tea for several long minutes. Allow the individual(s) to drink, all the while focusing on the intention and the burning of the candles. Try not to sweeten the tea, but if it is requested, serve coconut sugar. After the individual(s) are done and have exited, collect the steeped tea and wrap it in a cheesecloth. Allow the candles to burn out. Once the blend has dried, burn it, separate the ashes, and bury them in different locations.

Truth Tea

Use when you are in need of the truth from someone. You must share a pot of tea with the person in question. Before they step into your home, ignite a white candle by the entrance door. Open windows, and burn an equal blend of dragon's blood resin, white copal, frankincense, myrrh, and sandalwood over a charcoal patty. Fan this out over the area, then place by the back door to dispel lies. Boil your water in a cast-iron kettle. Blend together your recipe in a cast-iron cauldron.

1 teaspoon dandelion root

1 teaspoon dandelion leaf

2 teaspoons red clover

2 teaspoons borage flowers

Take this dry blend first to the white candle by the entrance. Hover and chant:

Truth will only be welcomed.

Then take the blend to the burning incense at the back door. Hover and chant:

Lies will only be banished.

Now drop 1 tablespoon of the tea blend into a traditional cast-iron teapot. Brew it strong, between 8 to 10 minutes. Almond milk may be added after serving the tea.

Encourage everyone to finish all their tea. Then begin to ask your questions casually, working them into the conversation nonchalantly. You shall have the truth.

Beauty Tea

You will need:

A white teapot
A teapot warmer
A vanilla tealight candle
Fresh rose petals
1 teaspoon blue vervain
½ teaspoon anise seed
2 teaspoons rose hips
1 sprig fresh rosemary
1 to 2 sugar cubes
Fresh cream

Boil a pot of water, and as it is boiling, prepare the space. Place your teapot on the warmer with a vanilla tealight. Blend your recipe in the strainer in the teapot. Hover your hands over the herbs and visualize a golden aura infusing them. Picture this aura as the radiant beauty of a goddess of your choice. Or you may visualize the essence of what beauty means to you. Breathe your spark of life into the tea. When ready, pour the hot water over the tea and brew for 5 minutes. As the tea is steeping, encircle the teapot and warmer with the fresh rose petals clockwise. Then light the tealight within the warmer.

Chant four times:

Sweet as fresh cream,
Infinite beauty shines through me.

Pour a cup and add sugar and cream. Enjoy the rest of the pot of tea with some lovely vanilla scones or rose petal shortbread.

Courage Tea

If possible, use a cast-iron kettle to boil your water when making this tea. This tea spell is best done with one lit white or orange candle nearby your favorite large and thick mug. The courage sigil shall be carved into the candle and drawn with a chalk marker on the mug. Blend your recipe within the mug, lightly wave your fingertips over the candle flame, then hover your hands over the herbs. Envision the rays of the sun shining bright within the darkness, its warm and heated embrace waiting to be consumed. Give the tea blend life with your breath.

> 1 teaspoon black tea
> 1 teaspoon chamomile
> 1 teaspoon yarrow
> 1 sprig fresh thyme

Boil your water, then brew a nice strong tea for 7 to 8 minutes.

As it steeps, chant seven times:

> *I am brave, and I am fair.*
> *I have no fear or despair.*

Drink or serve when courage is needed. Instills fortitude when facing any challenges. Almond or walnut milk may be added.

Friendship Tea

From beginning to end of this ritual, you must begin to think about what it means to have friends in your life. Imagine the friendships you are seeking. Let this tea serve as a beacon and offering to attract friends to you. You will need:

A pink tealight candle
Almond oil
1 pink ribbon
2 white ribbons
A white or pink teapot with strainer
Teapot warmer
1 teaspoon oolong tea
1 teaspoon hibiscus
1 teaspoon jasmine
1 dash lemon zest
1 teaspoon honey

Anoint the pink tealight with the almond oil. Envision yourself laughing with friends and finding comfort. Light your candle and place it in the teapot warmer. Weave together the pieces of ribbon while calling out the values that make a friendship strong and trustworthy. Once done, tie this braid around the rim of the teapot. Imagining this bond bringing friends to you. Within the strainer, blend your tea. Breathe into the pot your spark of life and essence. Heat a kettle of water to 195 degrees and pour the water into the teapot. Let brew for 3 to 5 minutes. Strain and serve with honey. Enjoy your tea slowly, till the tealight is extinguished, envisioning the perfect friendship coming to you.

Mental Clarity Tea

This tea is ideal to drink before work or school, or during the waxing moon to keep a clear and steady mental flow.

Try to obtain a green or yellow mug to brew your tea in, and a white chalk marker. Upon the outside of the mug, you will need to draw an open eye. Heat a cup of boiling water. Within the mug, blend your recipe. Breathe into the cup, then hover your hands over the herbs and focus on your intent.

1 teaspoon mint
1 teaspoon lemon verbena
1 dash yellow mustard seed
1 sprig fresh rosemary
1 slice lemon
1 teaspoon honey

Pour the hot water over the tea blend, add the slice of lemon last, and as it is brewing, stare deeply into the mug. Breathe and meditate. Visualize your inner eye opening. Sweeten with 1 tsp of honey and use the fresh sprig of rosemary to stir clockwise. Lift up to your face and inhale the tea's aroma and energy.

Chant four times:

As rosemary is free, and mint brings cheer,
My mind is blessedly clear.

Sip the tea after each chant.

Healing Tea

It is recommended to do this spell bimonthly, preferably during the new and full moons, to renew the body's ability to heal itself.

1 teaspoon saffron
1 stick cinnamon
½ cup apple cider
honey

Brew the saffron and cinnamon stick in a white cup half-filled with hot water. Add in as much honey as you like. Stir in the apple cider clockwise with the cinnamon stick when the tea has cooled ever so slightly. As you stir, chant:

Sweet apple orchards,
Grow strong and vital.
As will my health,
Grow unyielding and capable.

Delicious when served over ice as well.

Psychic Eye Tea

1 teaspoon lemon balm
1 teaspoon peppermint
1 teaspoon yarrow
⅛ teaspoon mugwort
¼ teaspoon whole cloves
1 stick cinnamon

To awaken and discover your psychic abilities, this tea shall be brewed and drunk when the moon is full. You must be able to sit comfortably in a room, where it is silent, with a white candle burning and a crystal ball. Blend your tea within your cup and brew for 4 to 5 minutes. Strain and drink. Darken the room enough that only the candlelight is illuminating the crystal ball. Ground yourself, then sit up straight. Channel your energy through your body and calm your mind. Grasp the crystal ball between your hands and charge it with your energy. Then set it back on its stand while keeping your focus and maintaining the connection. Relax your gaze and find a spot on the crystal ball that calls to you. Bring all your attention to that spot. Leave your mind open and don't hold on to any preconceptions that may arise. You should begin to feel a vibration within your connection. Tap into this and focus on what you feel, hear, or see. Visualize yourself having no borders or edge—simply a long stretch of white light. Be sure to note down anything you sense, and once your eyes grow tired, take a break, and sip on more tea. Rest and breathe. You may try again after a while. This is an ideal remedy to practice with this tea blend to continue to tap into your psychic awareness.

Hex-Breaker Tea

The one tea you will not be drinking! This remedy is best when done any time between the waning and new moons.

You will need:

A cauldron

1 white taper candle in a heavy candleholder

Equal parts of:

elder flower

milk thistle

vetiver

lavender

Place the white candle in the heavy candleholder and set it in the middle of the cauldron. In a counterclockwise manner, encircle the candle with each of the herbs. Hover your hands above and set your intentions. If you know the one who has hexed you, focus on their face. Spit into the cauldron. Slowly fill the cauldron with water, just enough that the candle extends above the waterline. Light the candle and visualize the hex being broken.

Chant thirteen times:

Hexes will be drowned,
Hexers will be bound.
When the spell breaks,
You shall learn from your mistakes.

As soon as the flame burns down and touches the water, it will go out. Immediately take this out and dig a hole in the earth and pour in the broken hex and bury the candle.

Rise and walk away. Do not look back.

Silver-Tongued Tea

Prepare your space with a burning silver-colored candle and a silver dish. It is recommended to anoint the candle with sunflower oil.

Blend together in the silver dish:

> 1 teaspoon oolong tea
> ⅛ teaspoon fenugreek seeds
> 1 to 2 dried dandelion blossoms
> 1 small piece ginger

Hover your hands over the dish and chant:

> *My voice be heard, my words understood.*
> *By my command, all will come true.*

Boil your water to 180 degrees in a silver kettle and brew this recipe for 3 to 4 minutes. Strain and carry in a silver thermos. Drink right before delivering an important speech or interview, or to persuade people with your words. Enhance this spell by chewing on more candied ginger pieces after sipping on the tea.

Tea for a Broken Heart

You will need:

Sea salt
2 pink candles
2 purple candles
A clear quartz
A rose quartz
A glass bowl
Glass teapot
A glass cup
1 teaspoon black tea
1 teaspoon white willow bark
1 teaspoon milk thistle
1 teaspoon lavender
1 star anise
1 teaspoon violet blossoms
1 teaspoon mullein
1 to 2 teaspoons honey

It is recommended to do this spell on a Friday morning or evening. Mix the sea salt in a hot bath and soak for however long you feel is needed. Afterward, prepare the space by placing the teapot and bowl at the center of the altar. Arrange the two pink candles north and south, and the two purple candles east and west. Grant yourself plenty of space to stand within them. Begin to blend your herbs in the glass bowl. Place the sterile clear and rose quartz over the tea. Bring a kettle of water to boil. Once ready, enter your space with the kettle and light the candles clockwise, starting from the north. Visualize a healing and loving energy filling the space. Remove the crystals and place on either side of the teapot. Pour your tea into the teapot then let brew for 10 minutes. As it is steeping, hover your hands over the pot.

Chant:

> *Black is the day in which it bleeds,*
> *Torn away to the weeping well.*
> *Milk the thistle to receive its ease,*
> *Over lavender's hopeful spell.*
> *Blown to dust is the star,*
> *With the promise of blossoms from afar.*
> *And to forget mullein's fateful blight,*
> *To which soothing kisses*
> *Reach the cold places at night.*

Strain and pour yourself a cup of tea. Add honey to sweeten. Sip slowly, visualizing love and warmth entering your heart. You may sit quietly, focusing on the candles lit around you, to the promise of healing and where you see yourself in the future. When you are done with your tea, snuff out the candles and close your space. You may repeat this spell every Friday until the heart has mended.

Moon Teas and Esbats

ere are the recipes that honor the phases of Grandmother moon. Brew them accordingly to influence Her energies into your day-to-day life. Celebrate them during Her powerful hour or offer the tea as a symbol of admiration. Discover which of Her moon phases sway you the most. Align your nature to Her ascendancy and command your magick.

It is good to bless the fresh herbs under the moonlight, in Her proper phase, to gather their strength as future moon teas. Choose a devoted pot for these teas and paint upon its surface with a heat-safe paint the symbol of the moon. If this pot be made of cast-iron, all the better—iron is a symbol of strength and unity. Before the first use, rinse and gently clean the pot, then infuse thoroughly with warm moon water only (see page 149). Do not use soaps or detergents. Wipe the outside dry with a clean cloth while the pot is still warm and allow to air dry.

Within this chapter you'll find esbat rituals for each of the moons of every month, which are used to honor full-moon gatherings, and to symbolically attune your life.

The moon in all Her glory
Blesses a good-rounded teapot.

New Moon Tea

1 teaspoon black tea

1 teaspoon blue mallow

1 slice lemon

1 teaspoon coconut milk

For defense spells, warding off evil, and rejuvenation, as well as new beginnings and personal improvement.

Waxing Moon Tea

1 teaspoon white tea

1 teaspoon lemon balm

1 teaspoon dried papaya bits

1 teaspoon coconut sugar

For drawing spells, such as for luck, love, and new opportunities, as well as protection.

Full Moon Tea

1 teaspoon green tea

1 teaspoon jasmine

1 teaspoon chickweed

1 teaspoon coconut milk

For abundance spells in love, health, and success.

Waning Moon Tea

1 teaspoon oolong tea

1 teaspoon willow bark

1 teaspoon marshmallow root

1 teaspoon coconut sugar

To banish, thwart, and ward negativity, as well as for divination spells.

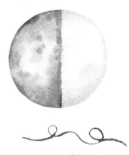

Blue Moon Tea

¼ teaspoon mugwort

¼ teaspoon goldenrod

1 teaspoon blue mallow

1 teaspoon mullein

2 teaspoons honey

Ideal would be to drink during a powerful blue moon for it instills wisdom, money, divination, astral travel, courage, banishing, fertility, healing, health, love, prophetic dreams, prosperity, protection, enhancing psychic powers, and strength.

Eclipse Tea

1 teaspoon pu-erh tea

1 teaspoon dried lemon peel

1 teaspoon dried orange peel

1 vanilla bean

1 teaspoon honey

To instill the powers of the moon and sun into yourself. For all matters of luck, strength, courage, abundance, harmony, healing, transformation, wish magick, and conjuring.

Tea of the Stars

1 teaspoon Assam black tea
1 star anise
1 teaspoon dandelion root
1 stick cinnamon
1 to 2 teaspoons date sugar
Splash of hazelnut milk

To drink on nights when the stars shower across the skies. Good for wishing spells.

Barley Moon Tea Esbat (January)

You will need:

3 white candles
A white altar cloth
Handful of clear quartz
A clear glass teapot
Cinnamon incense
Gardenia oil

Wear white clothing of the coziest material that's warm for the occasion. The hair may be wrapped in a white scarf. Jewelry may be of wooden or other natural substances. Boil a pot of water and as it heats prepare the space. Spread out the altar cloth and place the three white candles at the top. Have the teapot at the center. Encircle the teapot with clear quartz. Anoint the candles, then your hands, feet, and third eye. Light the candles and incense.

Blend together:

3 parts roasted barley
1 part ginger
Splash of milk

Brew for 7 minutes, all the while chanting:

The cold moon does not settle in the bones,
nor does it freeze us in place.
We are open to purification, and new beginnings we embrace.

Salute to the energies around you, sweeten your brew, and drink the tea slowly. Foresee a bright new road ahead and open yourself to the greater possibilities. Continue the ritual with spells for manifestation, inner self-purification, protection, stability, or healing.

Parsley Moon Tea Esbat (February)

You will need:

A wool altar cloth
Six colors-of-the-rainbow candles
A few budded twigs in a vase
An earthen mug

Blend together:

1 teaspoon pu-erh tea
1 teaspoon dried lemon peel
1 teaspoon dried orange peel
Pinch of parsley
1 vanilla bean

For this ritual, you may wear flowing clothing and ribbons of numerous colors, bright amulets, budded crowns of flowers, and many rings on your hands and feet, and remain barefoot. Boil your moon water for your tea and steep for 2 to 3 minutes. Surround your tea mug with the budded twigs in a circle. Hover your hands over the circle and when the mind is clear grasp the warm mug.

Chant:

Rainbow goddess of stormy skies,
bring me new seeds to grow and rise.
And I shall tend to them and bring new life,
So that they could end all strife.

Sip on your tea as you envision what new opportunities you wish to grow in your life. You may continue the ritual with spells for ambition, enlightenment, astral travel, healing, purification, love, and new beginnings.

Thyme Moon Tea Esbat (March)

You will need:

A yellow altar cloth
12 yellow candles
1 yellow ribbon
1 sound bowl
Sandalwood incense
Coconut oil
Teacup with gold rims (if possible)

Blend together:

1 teaspoon green tea
1 teaspoon jasmine
1 teaspoon thyme
1 teaspoon shredded sweet coconut
Splash of coconut milk

You may wear yellow and light fabrics, and little jewelry with a few gold rings. Boil moon water to 160 degrees and steep for 1 to 2 minutes in a teapot. Strain. Set up the altar and arrange the candles throughout the space. Apply the oil onto your wrists and feet, then burn the incense. Light the candles. Serve yourself a cup of tea, then hover and ring the brass bell over the teacup.

Chant:

> *Upon this night, I rejoice and vow,*
> *that I am glittering light, and my power is unbound.*
> *With this ribbon and with this tea,*
> *I seal these words by the power of three.*

Take the ribbon and knot it three times around the teacup's handle. Drink to your newfound power. You may continue the ritual with spells for renewal, reconciliation, balance, growth, prosperity, and new beginnings.

Basil Moon Tea Esbat (April)

You will need:

A green altar cloth
2 green candles
Balm of basil
Clear glass teacup and bowl

Blend together in the bowl:

1 teaspoon mint
1 teaspoon hibiscus
1 teaspoon juniper berries
Pinch of basil

You may wear green and white garments, and silver jewelry or a small moon amulet.

Boil your moon water and brew the tea for 5 to 7 minutes. Add honey and cream to desired amount. Place in the refrigerator for several hours, till slightly cooled.

Prepare the space. With the balm, anoint the candles and then yourself, especially the hands, feet, and third eye. Anoint all others who are in attendance. Serve tea over ice.

Chant:

New life springs forth and is reborn.
We too are renewed and adorn.
Silver light above the sky,
Instill in us the essence to be alive.

Toast to life and honor the moon by casting spells for new beginnings, fertility, prosperity, banishing bad habits, confidence, and opportunities through dance and laughter.

Honeysuckle Moon Tea Esbat (May)

You will need:

A blue altar cloth
2 blue candles
Blue flowers in bloom
Small dish of honeysuckle and lilac oil
Glass teapot
Honey jar

Blend together:

4 parts dried violets
3 parts white willow bark
2 vanilla beans
1 part dried honeysuckle flowers

You may wear various shades of blue garments and glittering jewelry of gold, silver, and crystals. Boil moon water. Prepare the space by setting up the candles at either side of the glass teapot in the middle of the cloth, then arrange the blue flowers around the area. Brew the tea for 5 to 7 minutes. Anoint the cloth, flowers, and candles with the oil. Then anoint your feet, hands, and third eye. Serve a cup of tea. Then, apply a small amount of honey onto your lips. Know that you will soon be honoring heaven and earth and the perfect balance of this night, as well as honoring the sacred feminine mysteries.

Relax and then meditate soundly. As you take a sip of your tea, focus in on the sweet decadence of the honey on your lips. Say out loud what you honor within yourself and what balance you seek to find in your life. This ritual is also an ideal time to spirit walk and/or enter the gates of the underworld. You may also continue the ritual to do spells for duality, personal growth, and expansion magick.

Lavender Moon Tea Esbat (June)

You will need:

A gold altar cloth
2 gold candles
2 light purple candles
Amber incense
Neroli oil
Handful of yellow agates
Fresh lavender bundles
A French press

You may wear large and overflowing garments of gold and purple. Create a lavender crown to place upon the head. Exquisite and broad jewelry of gold and heavy gemstone pendants must adorn the body. Anoint the hands, feet, and third eye with the neroli oil in a base. Bring a pot of water to boil, then prepare the space. Spread out the altar cloth and place your anointed candles in a decorative pattern across the space. Scatter the yellow agates across the altar. Place your French press at the center. Light the candles then the amber incense and smudge across the surface, including the candles, the French press, and yourself.

Blend within the French press:

1 part dried lemon slices
1 part dried orange slices
1 part dried cherries

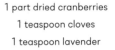

1 part dried cranberries
1 teaspoon cloves
1 teaspoon lavender

Pour the boiling water over your blend and steep for 8 to 10 minutes. As it is brewing, take in the scents and energy around it, the vibrancy of the candles, the incense, and the tea brewing. Breathe deeply and focus on the goals you had created for yourself at the beginning of the year. Have they been met? Do you seek more? Visualize the dreams you wish to see manifested in the next six months.

Chant:

> *Life's essence moves ever forward;*
> *So too shall my goals and dreams.*
> *Lavender's moon ignites what was most desired,*
> *And brings it forth upon moonbeams.*

Seal the spell by pressing down on the French press slowly. Serve it either alone or sweetened. Toast to your goals and dreams coming into reality. You may continue your ritual with spells involving clarity, enhancing, transformation, or fairy magick.

Jasmine Moon Tea Esbat (July)

You will need:

A dark purple altar cloth
2 white candles
2 purple candles
Frankincense resin
Pinch of cumin
Charcoal disk
Heat-safe bowl
A few white agates or opals
A white teapot and cup
A tea tray

You may wish to wear formfitting white, black, or dark purple garments, with small glittering jewelries adorning the body. Bring a pot of moon water to boil. Set the space by spreading the altar cloth down, then place the tea tray at the center, with the teapot and cup. Place your candles around this tea tray. Ignite the charcoal disk and place within the heat-safe bowl. Burn the frankincense and sprinkle the cumin over the resin. Blow gently upon the incense to produce a lot of smoke. Smudge the area, candles, and yourself. Place the incense bowl beside the teapot. Light the candles.

Within the teapot, blend:

1 part jasmine
1 part chamomile

1 part dried blackberries
1 slice dried lemon

Brew for 6 to 8 minutes. As it is steeping, waft your hands across the incense smoke then let it hover over the tea. Visualize a great white and purple aura illuminating throughout the space. Focus on this energy turning into steam and smoke then entering the body. See this energy mold into a protective and purifying shield within your essence.

Chant:

> *The jasmine moon is my strength and ally.*
> *Protection and love are by my side.*
> *The coming months are sanctified.*
> *Evil will have no choice but to abide.*

Seal this promise by toasting to the powers that be and drinking the tea. Add honey and cream to amplify the protection. Meditate on the energy of the tea as it purifies your heart and spirit, and especially your psychic senses. Moving forward, your mental, emotional, and spiritual essence shall be protected from evil entities. You may continue the ritual with shadow work, divination, or spells for long-term goals.

Rosemary Moon Tea Esbat (August)

You will need:

An orange silk altar cloth
4 orange candles
3 red candles
2 carnelian stones
1 green tealight candle
Glass teapot and cup
Teapot warmer
Dragon's blood incense stick and incense holder

You may wear highly decorated yellow, red, and orange garments, with gold, beaded, and black jewelry. You may also wear large healing talismans. Bring a pot of moon water to a boil. Prepare the space by spreading out the orange silk altar cloth. Place the teapot warmer at the center with the teapot and cup. Have the green tealight within the warmer, the carnelian stones on either side of the warmer stand, the red candles above those, and the orange candles at the very top of the altar space. Within the teapot, blend:

1 part black tea
1 part rose petals
1 part peppermint
1 part chamomile
1 pinch saffron threads (about 12 threads)

Pour the hot water over the blend and let steep for 5 minutes. Strain, then add a healthy amount of honey to sweeten.

1 sprig of rosemary
2 slices of lemon

Use the sprig of rosemary to stir clockwise. Leave the stem within the teapot. Now add the lemon slices. Ignite the incense, and while it is still aflame light the green tealight and chant:

Green is for the Heart.

Light the three red candles and chant:

Red is for the Body.

Light the four orange candles and chant:

Orange is for the Soul.

Blow out the incense and rest it upon the holder. Gently touch both carnelian stones on either side of the tea warmer and chant:

I am the life force of vitality.
My power and health are endless.

Serve yourself a cup and as you take the first sip and chant:

The Heart, the Body, the Soul,
Are one and healed.
The power within and the health as a whole
Are strengthened and shielded.

Enjoy the rest of the tea as you visualize your life force being flooded with renewed health, fire, and strength. You may continue with the rest of the ritual with spells for friendships, peace, reflection, cleansing, and harvesting.

Mugwort Moon Tea Esbat (September)

You will need:

A brown altar cloth

4 brown candles

2 white candles

A pine, lavender, and vervain bundle

A mug

Strainer

½ teaspoon mugwort

You may wear loose and comfortably worn brown or white clothing. No jewelry may be worn. The hair must be loose and the face clean. Bring a cup of moon water to a boil. Prepare the space by setting up your altar in the main area of the home. Spread out your altar cloth, then place your mug at the center. Place the two white candles on either side of the mug, then set the four brown candles on the outer edge, in a circle around the center items. Have the strainer set within the mug with the mugwort. Ignite the candles, starting with the brown ones, then to the white. Hover your hands over the mug and visualize the mug being your connection with your hearth. Focus on the mug becoming your doorway that links you with the energies of your personal space, a physical embodiment of your home. The home is a physical and magickal extension of yourself; what you put out around your space is what you're going to continuously sense and have flowing through it. A balanced home brings peace and joy. Use this ritual to bring yourself in touch and in alignment with your home.

You can either use the mugwort to enhance this connection, or you may simply drink the moon water alone. If using mugwort, brew for 5 minutes, then strain. You may sweeten with honey. Sit and meditate, visualizing yourself connecting with your home, becoming your space. You may use this time to speak words of love and encouragement to your house. When ready, ignite the herb bundle and smudge yourself, focusing on your home and hearth being cleansed as well. You may also choose to move around and smudge each room, while continuing to speak words of kindness and joy. You may continue your ritual with spells for love and relationships, psychic work, and reflection.

Sage Moon Tea Esbat (October)

You will need:

A silver altar cloth
4 silver candles
1 white candle
Sweetgrass
A sage and bergamot balm
A silver metal kettle
A large glass cup
Strainer
1 tablespoon roasted dandelion root

You may wear silver or white garments, with large black shawls or robes, and long, flowing silver jewelry. You may especially favor silver glittering headpieces and bells around the ankles. Bring a few cups of moon water to a boil in your metal kettle. Prepare the space by spreading out the silver altar cloth, then arrange the four silver candles in each cardinal point. Anoint yourself with the balm of bergamot and sage, as well as applying this to the candles. Place the one white candle, large glass cup, strainer, and dandelion root at the center. Once the kettle is done boiling, bring it within your circle and place it on a heatproof mat beside your cup. Begin to light the candles, starting at the north point and lighting clockwise, ending at the west point. If you wish, you may use this time to call on the guardians of each direction and cast a circle. Light the center white candle and sit comfortably. You may also dedicate this candle to an individual deity.

Use the center candle's flame to ignite the sweetgrass and blow out to create an incense. Pour the hot water over the roasted dandelion root and brew for 8 to 10 minutes. Hover your hands over the cup.

Chant four times:

Guiding spirits, I call to you.
Clear away the noises with this brew.
Open the doorway to new sight.
I summon my gifts upon this night.

Strain and sip upon the tea. When ready, focus your sight on the surface of the metal kettle, treating it much like a mirror. Find the reflection of the candle's flame and scry deeply. Go into a trance state and dive deep. Study the shapes and sensations that you sense, feel, see, and hear. Take note of everything you discover. You may sense your guides' presence during this scry. When you do, this would be the ideal time to ask questions of the past, present, or future. After you receive your messages, pull away from your trance slowly, and close your eyes. Breathe in deeply and continue to sip upon your tea to reground yourself. Before closing your circle, you may continue your ritual with further divination and spells of wisdom, ancestral magick, ambition, and cleansings.

Yarrow Moon Tea Esbat (November)

You will need:

A black altar cloth
1 white candle
Heat-safe plate
8 snowflake obsidians
An oil burner
Wisteria and lilac with a base oil
1 bay leaf
A black and white mug
Strainer

You may wear worn out and dull black and gray garments that hang loosely. No jewelry may be worn; feet must be bare. Bring a cup of moon water to boil. Prepare the space by spreading out the altar cloth and placing the mug on the plate, with candle, oil, and burner at the center. Surround these items in a circle with the snowflake obsidians. Light the oil burner with the oil, then the candle.

Blend within your mug:

1 sprig of dried yarrow
1 teaspoon spearmint
½ teaspoon licorice root

Brew your tea for 5 minutes and as it is steeping, take the bay leaf with your right hand and lightly dip it into the oil within the oil burner.

Bring this bay leaf to your forehead as you hover your left hand over your steeping brew. Close your eyes and focus all your intentions on the bay leaf. Visualize releasing what you fear, doubt, and harbor deep within you on what you desire most to release.

Breathe out slowly. Chant:

I have the power within me to release what no longer serves me.

Then take the bay leaf and burn it over the white candle. Envision the bay leaf releasing these fears and doubts. Let it burn out on the plate next to your mug.

With your left hand still hovering over the mug, sense the energies surrounding the herbs and their ability to instill strength, clarity, and courage within you.

Breathe in deeply. Chant:

I have the power within me to accept the courage that will serve me through the hard and cold days ahead.

Take a sip of your tea and allow the spell to fill your body with renewed strength and courage. When ready, take the plate with the bay ashes out the back door and blow your faults to the wind. You may continue your ritual with spells for new beginnings, fidelity, protection, and connecting with the divine.

Wormwood Moon Tea Esbat
(December)

You will need:

Velvet red altar cloth
2 red candles
1 green candle
Frankincense and patchouli incense
Red sachet
Green felt-tip marker
Wooden bowl

You may wish to wear long garments of red or green, with dazzling gold jewelry. You may also choose to do this ritual beside your Yule log or Christmas tree. Prepare the space by spreading out your altar cloth and placing the bowl at the center. Ignite your incense. Then place the two red candles on either side of this bowl, with the green candle above it. Light your candles. Gather:

4 parts Earl Grey tea
3 pinches wormwood

Place these ingredients within your wooden bowl and smudge your incense over it clockwise. Then hover your hands above the blend. Breathe in deeply and visualize a radiant aura of red and emerald infusing the tea. Add to this vision sparkling specks of gold. Witness how attractive this energy is. Proceed to breathe your essence of life over the tea. Take hold of the red sachet and green marker and draw a symbol of prosperity and riches over both sides. Infuse these symbols with your energy as well. Then scoop the tea into this sachet. Use and brew a teaspoon of this tea every Tuesday thereafter to attract luck and prosperity to you. Sweeten with honey.

Horoscope Teas

avor these recipes of the zodiac. Each of the horoscope signs corresponds to different aspects of the human character. These star signs strongly influence personality, spirit, and emotions. By connecting with and understanding these elements through spell and ritual, you can shed light on your love life, career, and much more. It is recommended to discover your birth natal chart and explore which astrological sign is influential in your life, or which one is needed to balance out your energies.

Even Destiny takes a moment
to partake of tea with the Stars.

Aries Tea

Prepare a space at the table with a red cloth; red tealight; bloodstone, red jasper, and/or hematite; and the Emperor tarot card.

As the water heats to 200 degrees, prepare the tea.

Blend:

1 teaspoon black tea
⅛ teaspoon ground cardamom
⅛ teaspoon ground ginger
1 stick cinnamon

Brew the tea for 4 to 5 minutes.

As you drink the tea, focus onto the Emperor card. Meditate on the qualities and characteristics Aries possesses. Let their abilities of authority and analytical powers to help others and to achieve their goals empower your intentions for strengthening independence, generosity, passion, motivation, optimism, and courage. To soothe tempers, impulsiveness, and impatient behavior, and to aid in beginnings, and in sports of luck and talent.

Taurus Tea

Prepare a space at the table with a green cloth; a green tealight; aventurine, tiger's eye, and/or angelite; as well as the Hierophant tarot card.

As the water heats to 195 degrees, prepare the tea.

Blend:

1 teaspoon oolong tea
1 teaspoon dried plum pieces
1 teaspoon hibiscus
1 teaspoon rose hips

Brew the tea for 3 minutes.

As you drink the tea, focus onto the Hierophant card. Meditate on the qualities and characteristics Taurus possesses. Let their abilities of getting to the heart of every matter and seeing the important life lessons help you search for higher truths. To encourage determination, stability, strength of will, perseverance, artistry, and sensuality. To relieve stubbornness, inflexibility, and to increase your own powers.

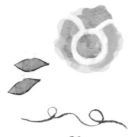

Gemini Tea

Prepare a space at the table with a yellow cloth; a yellow tealight; citrine, red jasper, or tiger's eye; and the Lovers tarot card. Heat a pot of water to 175 degrees.

Blend:

1 teaspoon white tea
1 teaspoon dried blueberries
1 teaspoon dried pomegranate arils
1 teaspoon licorice root
1 teaspoon bachelor's button

Brew the tea for 2 minutes.

As you drink the tea, focus onto the Lovers card. Meditate on the qualities and characteristics Gemini possesses. Let their abilities of adaptability, outgoingness, and positivity bring you balance toward deciding your personal path of integrity. To instill balance toward emotions and indecisiveness. To aid you in quickness of thoughts, energy, and wit. To help improves ideas and learning.

May also be used to soothe tempers between family members.

Cancer Tea

Prepare a space at the table with a silver cloth; a white tealight; moonstone, rose quartz, and/or carnelian; and the Chariot tarot card. Heat a pot of water to 175 degrees.

Blend:

1 teaspoon green tea
1 teaspoon dried raspberries
1 teaspoon dried apple bits
1 teaspoon jasmine
1 teaspoon hibiscus
1 teaspoon rose hips

Brew the tea for 45 seconds to 1 minute.

As you drink the tea, focus on the Chariot card. Meditate on the qualities and characteristics Cancer possesses: their sensitive and tenacious energy, how they combine their hearts and heads to persevere and overcome life's greater challenges, their ability to summon the right response and action when they are needed most. Brew this tea to embolden yourself with their intuition, loyalty, compassion, wisdom, and self-esteem.

May also be used to heal emotional pain and dependency, and release guilt.

Leo Tea

Prepare a space at the table with an orange cloth; a gold tealight; peridot, amber, and/or tiger's eye; and the Strength tarot card. Heat a pot of water to 195 to 205 degrees.

Blend:

1 teaspoon black tea
1 teaspoon saffron
1 teaspoon rose petals
1 teaspoon dried peach bits
1 teaspoon dried apricot bits
1 teaspoon dried pear bits

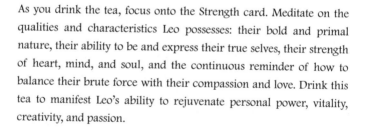

Brew the tea for 2 to 3 minutes.

As you drink the tea, focus onto the Strength card. Meditate on the qualities and characteristics Leo possesses: their bold and primal nature, their ability to be and express their true selves, their strength of heart, mind, and soul, and the continuous reminder of how to balance their brute force with their compassion and love. Drink this tea to manifest Leo's ability to rejuvenate personal power, vitality, creativity, and passion.

Cools stubbornness, arrogance, and over-indulging. Enhances personal magnetism and individuality.

Virgo Tea

Prepare a space at the table with a brown cloth; a green tealight; lapis lazuli, citrine, and/or carnelian; and the Hermit tarot card. Heat a pot of water to 195 degrees.

Blend:

1 teaspoon oolong tea
1 teaspoon rose hips
1 teaspoon marigolds
1 vanilla bean
1 teaspoon dried peach pieces
1 teaspoon honey

Brew the tea for 3 minutes.

As you drink the tea, focus onto the Hermit card. Meditate on the qualities and characteristics Virgo possesses: their cheerful and mental vigor, their ability to scrutinize when and how to share to the world their words, ideas, and feelings, their ability discover the treasure and mysteries the world can offer. Drink this tea to invigorate the senses. To restore cheerfulness, mental vigor, and efficiency. To mend short-temperedness, aloofness, and pessimism.

May also use when it involves work or service pursuits.

Libra Tea

Prepare a space at the table with a pink cloth; a light blue tealight; opal, topaz, and/or aquamarine; and the Justice tarot card. Heat a pot of water to 175 degrees.

Blend:

1 teaspoon white tea
1 teaspoon marigolds
1 teaspoon dried peach pieces

Brew the tea for 2 minutes.

As you drink the tea, focus onto the Justice card. Meditate on the qualities and characteristics Libra possesses: their inner truth, fairness, and ultimate balance, their ability to pay careful attention to the consequences and actions of themselves and others, and their understanding of the law of karma. Drink this tea to balance reason and confidence, to inspire creativity and seeing the bigger picture.

Drives away laziness, procrastination, and carelessness. May also be shared to bring understanding and strengthen a partnership. To influence a court case.

Scorpio Tea

Prepare a space at the table with a black cloth; a red tealight; obsidian, malachite, and/or citrine; and the Death tarot card. Heat a pot of water to 175 degrees.

Blend:

1 teaspoon green tea
1 teaspoon dried orange peel
1 cinnamon stick
1 small ginger piece
1 teaspoon fennel
1 teaspoon dried pomegranate arils
1 teaspoon cocoa nibs

Brew this tea for 45 seconds to 1 minute.

As you drink the tea, focus onto the Death card. Meditate on the qualities and characteristics Scorpio possesses: their power to continuously grow and detach from what no longer serves them, and their ability to make room for something new and to allow new opportunities to enter their lives. Drink this tea to nourish intuition, insight, and sensibilities, and stimulate the mental senses.

To ease trust issues, arrogance, complicated emotions, and stress. May also be used in lust and sex spells, prosperity spells and security, and in workings of deep spirituality.

Sagittarius Tea

Prepare a space at the table with a purple cloth, a purple tealight, turquoise, garnet, and/or blue lace agate, and the Temperance tarot card. Heat a pot of water between 195 and 205 degrees.

Blend:

1 teaspoon black tea
1 teaspoon bachelor's button
1 teaspoon blue mallow
1 teaspoon saffron
1 teaspoon dried mango pieces
1 teaspoon dried orange slices

Brew the tea for 2 to 3 minutes.

As you drink the tea, focus onto the Temperance card. Meditate on the qualities and characteristics Sagittarius possesses: their wisdom and understanding energy, their ability to combining strength and ultimate truth and awareness into the physical world. Drink this tea to encourage insight, optimism, and rationality, and enliven the spirit. May also be used to deter forgetfulness, rash decisions, and unintended actions.

Supports understanding, generosity, and helps in travel.

Capricorn Tea

Prepare a space at the table with a gray cloth; a black tealight; onyx, garnet, and/or smoky quartz; and the Devil tarot card. Heat a pot of water to 195 degrees.

Brew:

1 teaspoon oolong tea
1 teaspoon lemon balm
1 teaspoon marigolds
1 vanilla bean

Brew this tea for 3 minutes.

As you drink the tea, focus onto the Devil card. Meditate on the qualities and characteristics Capricorn possesses: their success and never-ending goals, their ability to tirelessly strive for eternal stability and security. Drink this tea to invigorate optimism, endurance, ambition, and sensitivity, and also to resolve inflexibility, misunderstandings, and alienating yourself.

Aids with luck spells and money, and improves communication skills.

Aquarius Tea

Prepare a space at the table with any color cloth; a blue tealight; amethyst, garnet, and/or aquamarine; as well as the Star tarot card. Heat a pot of water to 175 degrees.

Blend:

1 teaspoon white tea

1 teaspoon saffron

1 teaspoon bachelor's button

1 teaspoon shredded coconut

1 vanilla bean

Brew the tea for 2 minutes.

As you drink the tea, focus onto the Star card. Meditate on the qualities and power Aquarius possesses. Let their abilities of optimism and the belief of achieving your heart's desire wash over as you drink the tea, reminding you that your spiritual nature can make your greatest wishes come true. To flourish uniqueness, tolerance, independence, and forward-thinking. To calm rebellion and an accelerated nature. To aid in psychic abilities and personal powers.

Pisces Tea

Prepare a space at the table with a mauve cloth; a green tealight; aquamarine, moonstone, and/or rose quartz; and the Moon tarot card. Heat a pot of water to 175 degrees.

Blend:

1 teaspoon green tea
1 teaspoon dried pineapple pieces
1 teaspoon dried Mango pieces
1 teaspoon dried papaya pieces
1 teaspoon bachelor's button

Brew the tea for 45 seconds to 1 minute.

As you drink the tea, focus onto the Moon card. Meditate on the qualities and power the Pisces possesses. Let their abilities of strong intuition and compassion, and their strong desire to help others attune you to your deepest wisdom. To nurture patience, self-esteem, and dedication. To restore indecision, unrealistic outlooks, and trust issues. To aid in intensifying feelings of love in another. To draw good luck and protection.

Sabbat Teas

Revel in the witches' sabbats with ceremonial teas. Upon each of the sabbats, it is customary to serve a blessed beverage. This drink is to be dedicated to the theme of the night, after which a grand ritual has been concluded. Often a delectable brew, it is empowered with magickal properties to bestow within the drinker.

Follow these rites to connect and honor the sabbats that bond and join witches from around the world. A metal-lined copper teakettle will truly enhance the ceremonial ritual, and steeping the enchanted teas in a special pot of majesty or of rarity will deliver a most worthy experience. Serve the ritual tea to all present and be mindful of the magick it honors. These teas may also be used in dedication and offering to deities or the ancestors.

As the Wheel turns the Seasons,
So too
Can stirring a teacup bring change.

New Year's Day Tea

(January 1st)

A refreshing tea to begin a New Year. Begin this spell when the clock strikes midnight. Gather three white candles, a bowl of ice, and your tea blend. Light the candles and breathe deeply. Sit quietly and meditate on all the lessons learned and all the troubles you have faced this past year.

Blend:

> 1 teaspoon holy basil
> 1 teaspoon peppermint
> 1 teaspoon spearmint

Release the tea blend and your woes over the bowl of ice. Visualize the cool energy of the ice freezing away negativity and purifying it with good vitality. Cover the bowl with a clean cheesecloth and set in the refrigerator overnight. In the morning of the new year, strain and drink. Take in the refreshing taste of a new beginning and a blessed coming year.

Imbolc Tea

(February 1st)

Use this tea as an offering during the grand sabbat of Imbolc/Candlemas.

Gather a very large bowl of water, a few floating candles, a spiral trivet, a white plate, and a teapot. Sit out in the garden with a cozy blanket and set up your space.

Blend:

1 teaspoon mint

2 teaspoons dried blackberries

1 teaspoon violet blossoms

¼ teaspoon bay leaves

1 teaspoon lavender

Place the trivet within the bowl of water and place your pot of tea upon it. Light your candles and dedicate your tea ritual to the goddess or to yourself. Sit in peace and say aloud your new affirmations for the coming spring.

Ostara/Spring Equinox Tea

(Varies from March 20th through the 23rd)

Gather a bundle of long willow withes, bound in a large circle with yellow, white, green, and light blue ribbons. Within this bundle set up a little altar of the same-colored candles and stones of aquamarine, citrine, and jade. Decorate with painted eggs, flowers, and jars. At the center, place a mixing bowl. Have an oil burner heating an oil blend of lilac, honeysuckle, and jasmine.

Within the mixing bowl, blend:

1 teaspoon white tea

1 teaspoon jasmine

1 teaspoon rose

2 teaspoons dried raspberries

Hover your hands over the blend and chant:

Blossom as nature breathes new life.
Fulfill with the life-giving light of the new sun.
Renew with the awakening of spring.

Fill the jars with this tea blend either for yourself or as gifts. Anoint the lids with the oil and place a stone from the altar on top. You may also paint symbols of new beginnings onto the jars.

Drink with a splash of coconut milk to celebrate the festival of rebirth where light and day are one.

Beltane Tea

(May 1st)

Use as a ritual beverage during the grand sabbat of Beltane when the Beltane fires are burning. The best bonfires for Beltane are ones where the nine sacred woods are brought together. It is especially enchanting to heat your pot of water over this sacred fire.

The nine sacred woods are:

Alder · Ash · Birch · Hawthorn · Hazel
Holly · Oak · Rowan · Willow

If possible, place your cast-iron kettle over the bonfire to boil.

Prepare your teacups and pot with braided ribbons of red, white, pink, green, and yellow. Wrap these around the handles or rims. Leave a tail of ribbon to flow in the wind.

Blend together:

1 teaspoon marigolds
1 teaspoon rose buds
2 teaspoons dried strawberries
Pinch lemon balm

Brew for 5 minutes and then serve with merry and cheer. You may add honey and almond milk. Make your pot of tea for yourself, friends, family, or community (double the recipe as needed).

Lithia/Summer Solstice Tea

(Varies from June 20th through the 23rd)

The best time and place to do this ritual is outside at noon, when the sun is at its peak. Gather multiple colors of roses and some sunflowers. You can also use carnelian, citrine, sunstone, tiger's eye, and quartz crystal. Bring your trusted cauldron to the center and begin creating a spiral pattern around it using the flowers and stones. In the surrounding area set large pillar candles of gold, yellow, or red. Have burning in a censer an incense blend of mugwort, chamomile, and lavender. Blend within a clean cheesecloth pouch:

1 teaspoon green tea

2 teaspoons dried cantaloupe melon bits

1 teaspoon elder flowers

1 teaspoon echinacea

1 fresh sprig rosemary

Place this large tea bag within the empty cauldron. Heat water to 175 degrees and pour it over the tea blend. Let it steep for 1 minute while you hover hands over the steaming cauldron and lift your face to the warm sun.

Chant:

The Sun's power collects its bounty and growth,
As the Earth accepts its fertile warmth.
We too shall rejoice and grow in their embrace and abundance.

Use a ladle to serve yourself and any others in attendance. Bless one another in the expansion of the season, and set your intention to manifest together bounty and growth. This tea can be used as well for any spells for protection, success, love, or healing. Or use in dedication rituals during the Midsummer's Eve ritual.

Lammas Tea

The best time for this ritual is just before the first harvest meal is served among family and friends. Set the table with your feast, leaving a center area cleared for a tea tray and a pot to brew. Around this center teapot, place your numerous baked breads, butters, corn husks, seeds, and strings. Blend within the teapot with a strainer:

1 teaspoon chamomile
1 teaspoon rose hips
2 teaspoons dried cherries
1 stick cinnamon

Brew the tea for 5 minutes; serve with milk and honey. As everyone sips, they shall then collect the corn husks, seeds, and strings to create their personal corn dolly. Within the heart of each dolly, place a few seeds and speak aloud of the kind of transformations you wish to see coming in your life. Or, you may speak of each gratitude you have in your life. When finished with the dollies, place them around the teapot and partake in the feast. Afterward, you may keep the dollies around the hearth for the rest of the season, keeping them safe and warm.

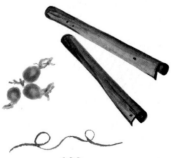

Mabon/Autumn Equinox Tea

(Varies from September 20th through the 23rd)

The best time to do this ritual is at sunset. At the center of your ritual space, place a very large wooden wreath and decorate it with bundles of rosemary, sage, and bay. You may also decorate the wreath with carnelian, citrine, obsidian, tiger's eye, and moss agate crystal. Place a beautiful, traditional cast-iron teapot at the center. Beside the wreath, collect a bundle of paper tags and have a pen on hand.

Place a strainer within the teapot, and in it blend:

1 teaspoon oolong tea
1 teaspoon chamomile
1 teaspoon dried apple pieces
1 stick cinnamon

Pour 195-degree water over the tea; let steep for 3 minutes. In a censer, burn an incense of sage, marigold, and myrrh. As the tea is brewing, each person in attendance may take a paper tag and write upon it a one-word wish, and clasping it between the hands, chant:

We give thanks to the bounty of Mother Earth.
May we too find our own bounty and wishes fulfilled.

Using string, attach the paper tags to the the wreath. Serve the tea, and toast to wishes granted, drinking to seal the spell and to accept these energies into yourself. Hang the wreath in the home or on the front door to attract these wishes into fruition. This recipe may also be used to celebrate Mabon, and harvest celebrations in general.

Samhain Tea

The third and final harvest feast is a time to honor our ancestors and pay our respects to elders, family members, and loved ones. Set the space with a large black cloth with a cleansed glass bowl in the center. Surround the bowl with four white candles. Burn incense of mugwort and sandalwood.

Blend within the bowl:

> 1 teaspoon red rooibos
> 1 teaspoon dried cranberries
> 1 teaspoon pumpkin seeds
> 1 stick cinnamon
> 1 teaspoon whole cloves

Place your cleansed hands in the bowl and imbue the tea blend with your energy and essence. Visualize the long roots of your lineage and ancestry flowing through you into the blend. When is done, take a tablespoon of the blend to an infuser (or double the amount for a pot of tea). Surround the brewing pot with smoky quartz and obsidian stones. Heat your water to 208 degrees. Cover the blend with water and hold your hands over the brew. Focus your intent on rebirth and transformation, filled with wisdom and recognition. Brew for 5 to 6 minutes. Just before serving, recite this blessing to all present:

> *Now as the veil between worlds thins,*
> *We call upon our ancestors to usher in.*

A time of great wisdom and to days gone by,
Toward new beginnings and for powers that mystify.
Though life retreats and the ground grows cold,
We honor the rebirth of traditions long olde.
May we face our shadows and transform anew,
Scry now as to the future and hold it true.

Add the stick of cinnamon to your pot last, or as a garnish. Add maple milk and sweeten with honey if you wish. Serve the pot of tea, sipping and absorbing your blessing. Partake of a feast together with gratitude and laughter. Hold séances or practice divination with all present. Keep the candles lit or ignite a bonfire and let it burn well into the night. Embrace and sing to the dear departed ancestors, especially as the midnight hour nears and the veil between worlds closes, and our loved ones make their journey.

To make the maple milk: heat a cup of milk and add 1 to 2 teaspoons of maple flavoring or syrup. Bring to a simmer and stir for a minute or two.

This recipe may be also be used for any other rituals on the grand sabbat of Samhain.

Yule/Winter Solstice Tea

(December 21st)

To bond with the Spirit of Light, here is a wishful tea ritual. Set the space with a sparkling white altar cloth with three blue and three white candles. Use a purified glass bowl to hold your herbs, and a teakettle for the water. If you truly wish to follow the old ways, it is said that the first full moon after Yule is considered to be the most powerful moon of the whole year. If you wish, you may do this tea ritual then.

Blend:

1 teaspoon black tea
2 tablespoons dried apricot bits
2 tablespoons dried figs
1 dash ground nutmeg
1 stick cinnamon
1 vanilla bean

As you blend each herb within your cleansed bowl, imbue the mix with your energy and intentions. Bring the cinnamon stick and whole vanilla bean together and visually bind them toward yourself with a long white string to create a wishing wand. Light the white and the blue candles and place them surrounding your bowl to empower the blend. Add a tablespoon of the blend to an infuser (or double the amount for a pot of tea) and surround the pot with clear quartz and/or emeralds. Heat your water to 205 degrees. Cover the tea with water and hold your hands over the brew. Focus your intent on what you wish for the season, filled with harmony and abundance. Brew for 5 to 6 minutes. Leave the wishing wand within your vessel. Add milk and sweeten with honey if you wish and use the wand to stir clockwise to activate the spell.

Just before serving, recite this blessing:

As the winter cold rushes in,
And we are put to rest,
May our dreams find their reality,
And our wishes blessed.
The Sun shall bring them into the light,
To await our warm awakening.
And there, we shall find
Our wishes calling.

Serve the tea; while sipping absorb your blessing.

Partake of this ritual with others with gratitude and laughter. Practice divination for the future. Cast spells for new beginnings, house blessings, and release. Keep the candles lit well into the night.

Blooming Teas

looming teas are a wonderful asset to have in the cupboard for any tea witch. A blooming tea is a step beyond a simple tea blend because it visually represents a spell coming into fruition. To create a blooming tea, you'll gather a bundle of young tea leaves and tie them together with a beautiful floral assembly. This is then bundled into a small ball and dried to contain its shape. Upon brewing, the ball unwraps—literally "blooming" as it brews—revealing the majestic nature of the tea. The result is a lovely and magnificent display of magick manifesting before your eyes.

For any tea witch, it is a high skill to learn how to create your very own blooming teas at home. You are essentially creating your own spell to bloom into the world.

Blooming teas can be made from most loose and leafy material, not just from young tea leaves. You may choose to use dandelion leaves, mint leaves, basil, violets, honeysuckles, clovers, and more. The best material for blossoming tea balls are flowers and plants that are entirely edible. When you are choosing, or foraging, pay attention to the life cycle of the plant or flower. Young leaves will deliver a lighter taste. If you choose older leaves, you will get a stronger flavor.

Any fresh plants or flowers you collect will need to be dried, either outside, inside, or in an oven or dehydrator no hotter than 100 degrees. A higher temperature will take away the aroma and flavor of the plants. After drying, preserve your plants in an airtight container away from light, moisture, and oxygen, until you are ready to create your blooming tea balls. Do not use moldy or wilted plants.

A needle

Pure natural-fiber thread, such as 100 percent cotton or hemp

5-inch square cheesecloth

Scissors

⅛ inch stem of small leaves

⅛ inch stem of large leaves

Flower blossoms with 1 to 2 inches of stem still attached

ASSEMBLY

To begin, select about 5 of the larger leaves—you will use these as the outside wrap of the ball. Split these leaves in two portions, reversing one portion so that you have leaf tips facing upward on all sides. Arrange the smaller leaves within this bundle, and use the thread to tie the bunch together at the center. Fan out the leaves in a sort of X and then shape the leaves into a cup. Use more thread to hold the cup shape at the bottom of the bundle. Take your threaded needle and sew through the head of the blossoms, straight through the stem, then through the center of the bundle, and knot it off at the bottom. Continue to sew in all the blossoms. Shape the leaves around the flower bundle and remove the thread that held the cup shape. Shape the leaves into a ball, and trim off any excess leaves. Wrap the ball tightly in the cheesecloth and tie a knot at the top. Then either place it in your oven or dehydrator, or hang it up until it is completely dry. Once dry, remove it from the cheesecloth and place it in an airtight container.

BREWING

Treat each of your blooming teas as a spell. Infuse your ball with your intentions and desires. Set the space, and always use a glass teapot. Boil your water and pour the hot water over your tea ball. As the blooming tea is steeping, focus fully on your spell and intentions. Visualize and pay attention to the tea as it blooms your magick into the world. When the tea ball has fully opened, the brew is ready to be drunk.

MAGICKAL FLOWERS

These flowers may be used with intention to create your blooming tea.

Carnation—Protection. Strength. Healing.

Chrysanthemum—Protection. Longevity.

Honeysuckle—Money. Psychic Powers. Protection.

Jasmine—Love. Money. Prophetic Dreams.

Lavender—Love. Protection. Longevity. Purification. Happiness.
    Peace. Prophetic Dreams.

Lilac—Exorcism. Protection.

Lily—Protection. Breaking Love Spells.

Marigolds, Calendula—Protection. Prophetic Dreams. Legal
    Matters. Psychic Powers.

Pansy—Love. Divination.

Peony—Protection. Exorcism.

Rose—Love. Psychic Powers. Healing. Love. Divination. Luck.
    Protection.

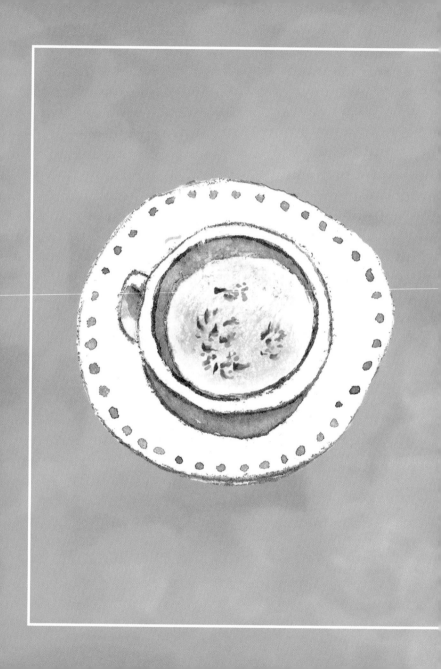

Tea Divination

ivination and the ceremony of tea drinking has always held a special place in traditions and cultures across the world. In the pantheon of divination methods—tarot, rune casting, and palm reading—the art of tea leaf reading holds a time-honored place. Reading tea leaves—called tasseography or tasseomancy—is one of the oldest known forms of divination. Passed down largely through oral tradition, the art of tasseography has historical roots in ancient China, the Middle East, and ancient Greece, and the practice probably spread around the world along with the tea trade. It's a divination method that is passed down through generations. Tasseography is a divination method using tea leaves, coffee grounds, or even wine markings to interpret patterns in a cup or glass. How the leaves are interpreted can see into the past, present, and future of an individual.

Tasseomancy is a practice full of ritual and ceremony. Practitioners generally have their own special kettle, teapot, cup, tools, and especially a special blend of tea to use. I have always loved using Tie Guan Yin oolong tea as my preferred leaves to read, along with my dear handed-down whistling kettle, my white teapot with a copper warmer, and the tasseography teacup my husband gifted me over eight years ago.

The ritual begins when the kettle is filled with water. Moon water is most recommended when it comes to divination. In the olden days, a stoked fire was also key to good divination work. The sound of the burning logs signals whether good or bad news is ahead. If the logs are quiet and humming, calm energy surrounds the reading. If they crackle, then the energy is tense and nervous. If they pop, then chaotic energy may be on its way. You must also always use a whistling kettle; the whistle acts as a ritual tool much in the same way as a ritual bell. It is a tool of invocation, used to banish negative influences, cleanse the space, and raise the vibrations at the beginning of a ritual. When the whistle blows, it is customary to let it sing as you say a blessing. Divination cups are always cleansed and washed thoroughly before use, then left to soak in cold water before air drying. They must be purified and cleaned at the end of every reading. The perfect cup is one with a handle, accompanied by a saucer. As hot water is poured from a dedicated teapot, you must treat the process symbolically. The teapot acts as your cauldron; it opens the doorway to the universe, the divine, the ancestors, and forms the connection between the brewer, the drinker, and the reading.

Set the space with the teacup and saucer in front of you, the teapot placed in the middle, and tea to the right. Use your teaspoon as a tool, much like a wand, to charge the tea, bestow blessings, and invoke the powers of divination. Drop the tea into the teacup, pour the hot water over the blend with intention, and allow to steep for 3 to 4 minutes. Then sit back and enjoy the tea with an open mind and heart. The drinker must drink with their dominant hand. Then, when the cup is nearly empty, swirl the tea that remains clockwise three times.

Clear your mind and tip the remaining tea into the saucer. Count to three then turn the cup back over. Study the leaf formations within the cup; the longer you look, the more your vision will open. Though the symbols have meaning, it is also important to trust your intuition and what your senses are telling you.

The positioning of the leaves is very important, as their placement reveals the directionality of your reading. You will begin the reading at the handle of the cup and scout out the symbols clockwise from there. The handle represents the Self and Home. Any symbols here will tell you about your personal well-being and the state of your home. From the handle to halfway around the cup, the rim represents the past. From halfway around the cup back to the handle, the rim represents what is taking place in the present. The middle section all around the cup represents the near future. The very bottom of the cup represents the distant future; or, if the drinker has one question, this part of the cup may be used to reveal the answer to the question.

After the reading, the leaves may be discarded depending on how well the reading went. If it was a positive reading, the leaves may be dried and kept as a charm for the outcomes to be blessed or buried near the home. If the reading was negative, the leaves may be dried and burned, the ashes scattered away.

Following is a list of common formations you might see in the cup, along with their interpretation. This is but a brief listing; there are numerous books available on tasseomancy, which you may want to consult for a fuller range of symbols and meanings.

Symbols

Airplane: Long Journey

Anchor: Stability

Apple: Achievement

Arrow: News

Axe: Difficulties

Baby: Small Worries

Bag: Trap

Ball: Variable Fortune

Balloon: Party

Basket: Award, Recognition

Bell: Announcement

Birds: Good News

Boat: Visit

Book: Good News, Secrets

Bottle: Temptations

Broom: A New Home

Bush: Secret Opportunities

Butterfly: Fickleness of Friends

Candle: Help from Others

Cat : Gossip, False Friend

Chain: Wedding, Responsibility

Chair : Guest

Circle: Success

Clock: Medical Help

Clouds: Trouble

Coins: Money

Cross: Death, Suffering

Cup: Reward

Dagger: Danger

Dish: Trouble at Home

Dog: Good Friend

Door: Opportunities

Dots: Busy Schedule

Duck: Money

Eagle: Success

Egg: Success

Envelope: Good News

Eye: Be Cautious

Face: Change

Feather: Insincerity

Fence: Limitations

Fire: Achievement

Fish: Increase of Wealth, Good
Fortune

Flag: Danger

Flower: Love and Esteem

Fly: Domestic Annoyances

Forked Line: Decisions

Fruit: Prosperity

Gate: Opportunities

Goat: Enemies

Grapes: Good Health, Happiness

Gun: Strife, Danger

Hammer: Hard Work

Hand: Friendly Helper

Hat: Improvement

Hawk: Suspicion, Jealousy

Heart: Love, Romance

Horse: Good News

Horseshoe: Good Luck

Hourglass: Decide

House: Security, Safety

Insect: Minor Problems

Jewels: Gifts

Kettle: Minor Illness

Key: Prosperity, but Be Cautious
Who Is Let In

Kite: Ascent in Social Positions

Knife: A Broken Friendship

Ladder: Advancement

Lamp: Secrets Revealed

Leaf: Change in Health

Letter: News

Lines: Progress, Change

Lion: Influential Friend

Lock: Obstacles

Man: Visitor

Moon: A Change in Plans

Mountain: Difficulties

Mouse: Stealing

Mushroom: Growth

Nail: Injustice

Necklace: Admirers

Needle: Recognition

Nest: Save Your Money

Octopus: Danger

Ostrich: Travel Abroad

Owl: Gossip Nearby

Palm Leaf: Victory

Palm Tree: Success

Parasol: New Lover

Parrot: Gossip

Pig: Greed

Pin: New Job

Pine Tree: Achievement

Pipe: Reconciliation

Pistol: Danger Is Near

Plow: Hard Going

Purse: Profit

Question Mark: Future Unsettled

Rabbit: Bravery

Rainbow: Better Days

Raven: Bad News

Rider: Good News

Ring: Marriage

Ring Broken: Divorce

Rose: Popularity, Romance

Scissors: Quarrels

Sheep: Good Fortune

Shell: Good News

Ship: Journey

Shoe: Change for the Better

Sickle: Illness, Sorrow

Snake: Enemy

Spider: Good Luck

Spiral: Creativity

Spoon: Generosity

Squirrel: Times of Want

Stairs: Success

Star: Happiness, Success

Sun: Joy, Success

Sword: Quarrels

Table: Social Gathering

Teardrops: Sorrow

Tortoise: Criticism

Tower: Disappointment

Triangle: Surprise

Turtle: Slow Progress

Umbrella: Protected

Violin: Self-Centered Person

Volcano: Harmful Words

Wagon: Wedding

Wasp: Romantic Problems

Waves: Travel

Wheel: Good Fortune

Wings: Messages from Heaven

Wolf: Cunning and Jealous

X: Stop, Wait, Listen

Zebra: Adventures Overseas

READ THE LEAVES WITHIN THE PALM

Another fun and quick method is placing a teaspoon of tea within someone's clean dominant hand and having them close it tightly. Have them breathe over the hand three times and open their palm wide. The placement of the leaves will reveal symbols and may be read. This is more for present readings or quick decision questions. If the answer is positive, that tea may then be brewed and consumed. If it is negative, burn the tea and dispel it from ever coming to be.

Potions

nrich your craft with the magickal properties of spirits. Discover the power within liqueurs by creating your own spirit blends and enjoying them during ceremony or other magickal acts. When brewing your potions, use bottles of glass. Paint upon the bottles the symbols of your desired manifestations, and when the bottles are filled, seal them with wax. Partake of these potions to gain wisdom or awareness, or to sooth the body and create well-being. One should drink these libations only with purpose unless you seek to confuse the sensibilities and muddle the original conjuring.

Please note that these potions, though liqueur and alcohol based, are very different from alcohol *tinctures*, which this grimoire presents in more detail beginning on page 146.

> *Offer your respect upon a kiss,*
> *To the Spirits that dwell within a cup.*
> *What secrets they may tell,*
> *And Hail!*

For the following recipes, pour spirits over all other ingredients in a tall, glass, airtight container. Seal the container, set aside, and do not disturb. Let the ingredients soak for 1 to 2 weeks, lightly shaking and turning the container over a few times once per day. Once the infusions are complete, strain the potion and store in an airtight container in the refrigerator for up to three months.

Solar Potion

For solar rites and sabbats. To manifest abundance, healing, protection, and love.

1 bottle tequila silver
6 whole limes
1 ½ cup lime juice
⅓ cup honey
3 pinches of sea salt

Drain the juice from the limes and then add to the container. You may add the peels as well, but that is optional.

Lunar Potion

For lunar rites. To summon fertility, mental powers, money, love, prophetic dreams, purification, wishes, and exorcism.

1 bottle peach Moscato
8 whole lemons
1 cup jasmine blossoms

Slice the lemons thinly and add to the container with the jasmine blossoms. Cover completely and let sit in the refrigerator for 4-8 hours before straining. Serve cold. Drink within 3 to 4 days.

Visionary Potion

For renewed intellect and vision. An excellent drink to serve among
company for understanding and communication.

1 bottle gin
1 bundle mint leaves
3 cucumbers (peeled, halved, and quartered)
3 splashes elder flower liqueur
2 to 3 limes (juiced)
⅓ cup simple syrup

Love Potion

To inspire love and lust. The cherries and peaches may be served to
further enhance the effects.

1 bottle rum
½ pound cherries (cut in halves)
3 to 4 peaches (cut in quarters)
1 pinch cumin powder
⅓ cup honey

Healing Potion

For healing and restored health. Enjoy over ice and club soda!

2 cups Everclear
4 to 5 apples (sliced)
3 sticks cinnamon
1 ¾ cup filtered water
¼ cup honey

Seal the jar and shake lightly. Refrigerate for 48 hours. Pour the mix through a mesh strainer and return the flavored vodka to the jar. Pour in the honey and filtered water and stir clockwise to fully combine. Seal tightly and store in the fridge. Good for up to 2 or 3 weeks.

Money Potion

For manifesting luck and money.

2 cups whiskey
3 cups fresh pineapple (cut into small chunks)
1 orange (sliced thin)
1 piece of ginger

Protection Potion

Drink or serve to manifest a circle of protection around the person.

1 bottle bourbon
1 bottle infused blueberry bourbon
2 cups fresh blueberries
6 lemons (sliced)
Handful of whole cloves
2 ½ cups honey
1 cup filtered water

Seal the jar and shake lightly. Refrigerate for 48 hours. Pour the mix through a mesh strainer and return the flavored bourbon to the jar. Pour in the honey and filtered water and stir clockwise to fully combine. Seal tightly and store in the fridge. Good for up to 2 or 3 weeks.

A Wishful Potion

To drink when there is a wish to be fulfilled. It also makes the perfect birthday gift.

1 bottle brandy
4 figs (halved)
1 vanilla bean
1 to 2 cups dandelion petals
Pomegranate seeds to garnish
¼ cup honey

Begin by putting the dandelion petals in a jar and pour the brandy over the petals. Seal the jar and shake lightly. Refrigerate for 48 hours. Pour the mix through a mesh strainer and return the liquid to the jar. Now add the figs and vanilla bean. Let sit for 1 to 2 weeks. Strain once more, discarding the figs and vanilla bean, and then stir honey in clockwise to fully combine. Seal tightly and store in the fridge.

Serve with pomegranate seeds. Add one seed per wish desired.

Cheers to Life

A potion to toast to life and all the riches it bestows. Perfect for celebrations of birth, weddings, and so forth.

1 ounce amaretto
1 ounce Grand Marnier
1 tea bag Earl Grey
1 orange twist
A pick of cherries

Brew 1 cup of Earl Grey tea; let cool. Add the amaretto and Grand Marnier. Garnish with the orange twist and cherries. Makes 1 serving

Cheers to Death

This is a two part recipe in which you'll be making your own homemade absinthe. You must savor this liquor slowly and in small amounts. Use only when honoring the dead, such as at a funeral or anniversary of the death, or in rituals that commune with the spirits.

Part one:

3 cups Everclear
⅓ cup wormwood (*Artemisia absinthium*)
⅓ cup anise seed
2 teaspoons (4 grams) fennel seed
4 teaspoons (8 grams) angelica root

4 cardamom pods
2 teaspoons (4 grams) coriander
2 teaspoons (4 grams) caraway
4 teaspoons (8 grams) star anise
2 teaspoons (4 grams) marjoram
½ seed of nutmeg
Filtered water

Purchase the dried organic ingredients separately and then blend. Add ⅓ cup of the herbal mix to 3 cups of Everclear. Make sure to store the mixture in a bottle and place in a warm, dark place. Let this infusion sit for between 2 weeks and 2 months.

Part two:

3 cups Everclear
2 cups hyssop
1 cup lemon balm
2 cups wormwood

In a separate bottle, infuse the hyssop, lemon balm, and wormwood in 3 cups of liquor. Let sit for a few days. Then strain the liquid. It should have a nice green color.

Combining:

Once the storage period of the first mixture is done, strain the herbs out. You will be left with a brown, bitter liquid. Distill this by boiling it. Alcohol will come to a boil at a lower temperature than water—

alcohol will boil at 175 degrees versus 212 degrees for water. When you infusion comes to a boil it will release vapor—this is the alcohol burning off. Bring it to a boil and when vapor starts rising, take the infusion off the heat and let it sit until it has cooled. This distilling process will take out the bitterness and some alcohol.

Add the second green-colored infusion to the distilled absinthe. Then add water to dilute, little by little, until the flavor is favorable.

Serve as one shot in a glass, place a stainless-steel absinthe spoon over the glass, and add a brown-sugar cube. Drip blessed moon water over the cube to dissolve it into the potion.

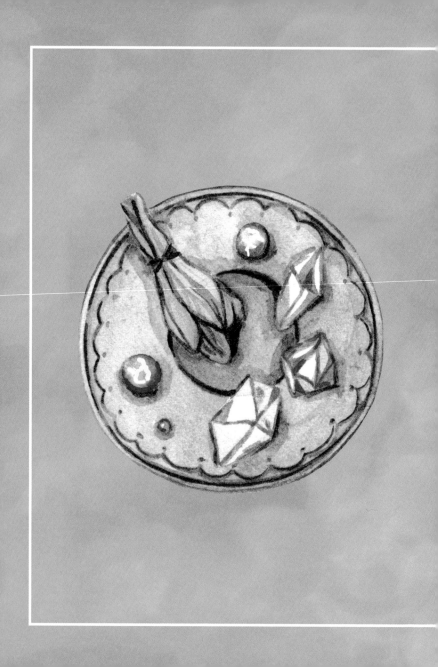

Empowering Your Tea

Your teas can be empowered in a number of ways. The two methods that I work with and recommend are using tea sigils and infusing your tea with the power of crystals.

Tea Sigils

Sigils are symbols that are painted, etched, drawn, or sewn over or into an object. That object is then bestowed with magickal power and intention. Sigils are used in spells to enhance the brewer's visualization and power, and to link them with the energies that be. Essentially, sigils "seal" the magick in. When it comes to tea witchery, sigils may be used to contribute more power into the remedies or rituals. Symbols may be drawn upon the teapot, teacup, saucers, teaspoons, tins, jars, tea tags—any physical part of the tea preparation. I personally love to use liquid chalk markers in different colors, depending on my intentions, and draw directly onto my teacup. (Note: do not draw inside the teacup—there are chemicals in the chalk or marker that you do not want to ingest!) These kinds of sigils can be easily cleaned away. Or, on occasion, I sew a sigil into a cheesecloth using clean cotton thread. I use these cloths to mold my blooming teas.

It is fun to create your own sigils. Let your intuition guide you. Consider deeply what remedy you need and then draw out the symbols that best reflect this to you. You can add symbols over symbols, in the end creating a large seal. Or you can keep it simple and write out a word instead. You can use glyphs for astrogical signs (see the section on Horoscope Teas) and even use Norse runes or Hebrew letters to create your sigil.

Here are the sigils I personally like to use, along with their meanings.

Circle: Movement. Balance. Journey. Road Opener.

Compass: Aid from All Directions.

Double Infinity: Unity of Opposites. Two Coming Together to
Create a Whole.

Eight-Pointed Star: Hope. Guidance.

Eye: Visions. Protection. Truth. Wisdom. Knowledge.

Flower: Romance. Innocence. Fidelity. Fertility. Positivity.

Heart: Love. Self-Love. Harmony. Peace. Beauty.

Infinity (Lemniscate) : Balance. Life. Death. Rebirth. Eternity.

Moon: Protection. Intuition. Psychic Abilities. Emotions.

Pentacle: Manifestation. Conjure. Spirituality.

Spiral: Transformation. Change.

Star: Hope. Luck. Opportunities. Happiness.

Sun: New Beginnings. Fresh Start. Success. Strength.

Sun and Crescent Moon : Wishes Fulfilled.

Tree: Prosperity. Life. Balance. Growth.

Triangle: Healing. Health. Good Fortune.

Tea and Crystals

The magickal properties of crystals have long held a place in the homes of many healers and witches, as part of their altars and daily lives. Crystals have long been believed to hold many kinds of healing properties and have the ability to transform energies. The terms "crystals" and "gemstones" are often used interchangeably but there is a distinction: a gemstone is a crystal, but a crystal is not always a gemstone. The presence of both crystals and gems lends powerful vibrations to a person, a space, or to magickal tools. For the workings of a tea witch, crystals are precious stones and gemstones that can be used to empower your herbs, tea tools, water, and spell remedies. Following is a list of water-safe crystals—you may get them wet, if necessary, or safely keep by or within your dry tea blend. Please be aware that, while these gems are water-safe, they should never be consumed internally. Don't even think about grinding a stone to powder in order to add it to your tea infusion! Crystals are only meant to lend their energy to your dry tea blend. If you place a crystal into the tea infusion itself, take it out before you consume the tea.

When you purchase any crystal or gemstone, it is important to immediately cleanse it before using it within your space or mingling it with other crystals. These stones absorb the energies of their surroundings and everyone who has ever touched them. You must make sure to neutralize and purify them before working them into your tea craft. It is always wise to thoroughly wash and sanitize your stones before consuming the strained water and tea they touch. In most cases, you may simply keep your stones beside the bowls, teapots, tins, and kettles without them physically soaking or touching your herbs. The choice is yours.

Cleansing, as opposed to washing, means you are clearing your crystals of any unwanted energy that may be stuck to them. Cleansing techniques include passing them through rainwater; smudging them; or letting them sit in moon water, sunlight, moonlight, earth or soil, or with purifying herbs such as bay, cedar, lavender, lemongrass, mugwort, peppermint, rosemary, sage, vervain, and witch hazel. Be sure to cleanse them often, especially after they have been handled by others, or when used in spellwork.

When you sanitize your crystals, it is important that you not use any chemicals or abrasive items. Simply wash them with mild soap and rinse with warm water, then allow them to air dry before storing them in a cloth bag or box. Avoid exposing stones to direct sunlight. Be certain that you do not use porous gemstones in your tea witchery.

The following are nonporous, water safe crystals, with descriptions of their attributes and uses.

AGATE

The good luck stone. This crystal offers protection and strength, and mentally enhances concentration and wisdom. It naturally balances the yin/yang energy and rebalances the mind, body, and soul, making it ideal to open and connect to the solar-plexus and crown chakras. It stimulates good health, pleasure, joy, and happiness within its environment, making this the most ideal gem to help free others from any bitterness they may be harboring, helping them come to terms with forgiveness and show compassion. This is also the perfect stone that can protect you from anything that may drain you mentally, emotionally, and spiritually. It may be used within your herbs, water, teapot, kitchen, and magick. Perfect to pair with chrysanthemums,

fennel, mint, and tea in protection, grounding, courage, and healing tea magick. It may be cleansed by any method. A really good self-sufficient stone.

AMETHYST

The ultimate spiritual, meditative, and calming crystal. It increases intuition and psychic powers. It encourages mental and emotional stability, strength, inner peace, and coping with loss or change, thus, also making it the perfect crystal to promote restful sleep, ease head tension, and support general healing and the immune system. It lends high vibrations to the third-eye and crown chakras. May be used within your herbs or beside your cups, teapots, and magick. It pairs perfectly with chamomile, lavender, and clove in anxiety, cleansing, psychic, sleep, peace, and protection tea magick. Amethyst should not be cleansed using direct sunlight, as sunlight can cause the stone to fade and become weak.

AVENTURINE

The stone of prosperity. This crystal delivers leadership qualities and promotes compassion and empathy. It is great to calm frustration and soothe anger. Protects against hasty decisions and rash responses. Delivers vitality, wisdom, and growth. Helps attract hope, joy, change, prosperity, and good fortune. Aids in the circulatory system and the general well-being of the heart, thus making it most ideal for the heart chakra. May be used in the herbs, on the tea altar, or beside the teapot. Perfect to pair with bergamot, tea, spearmint, and basil in money, prosperity, luck, and manifestation tea magick. May be cleansed with smudging or a pure water cleanse, but must not be left near heat or in the sun too long as it may affect the quality of the stone.

BLACK OBSIDIAN

The breaker-of-chains stone. This stone is most ideal to absorb negativity and cut emotional cords that block and inhibit growth, positivity, and the ability to move on. It aids in deflecting bad magick and any negative spells or entities that feed on energy. Clears the auric field, helps with self-control, and heals shock and trauma. Rebalances the digestive system, relieves joint pain, and releases addictions and bad habits. May also be used to protect and bring out the truth, to shatter illusions, and remove blockages. Stimulates and raises the root chakra. May be used within the herbs and on the tea altar. Best when paired with clove, lavender, yarrow, and sage in breaking spells, banishing, truth, and purification tea magick. This crystal should not be near any extreme cold or hot water temperatures or else it will break.

CARNELIAN

The vitality stone. This crystal has long been used in healing and in restoring vitality, creativity, and inspiration. It brings warm, joyous, and courageous vibrations. Mentally, it anchors people to the present while emotionally helping them accept and understand what it is that they need to cope with. It stimulates the circulatory, digestive, reproductive, and muscular systems. It balances and opens the sacral and solar-plexus chakras, thus making it an ideal stone for inspiring passion and sexuality. May be used in your herbs, beside the teapot, on stove tops, or in the center of the kitchen. Loves to be paired with cinnamon, cardamom, sage, and peppermint in creativity, mental focus, healing, and power tea magick. This crystal is not safe in salt water, so do not cleanse this gem with salt, otherwise it will be weakened and lose its vibrations.

CITRINE

The crystal of success. This gem is the perfect stone to draw success, prosperity, and abundance, especially in business or money matters. It also promotes wisdom, joy, and intellect, making it the most ideal stone to clear your mind, to easily tune into what the inner voice advises. It also dispels negative thoughts. It is rich with positive energies, making it a good companion to inspire and to keep one constantly motivated. Aids in bringing power and energy to the solar-plexus chakra. It may be used in your herbs, water, teapot, and magick. It loves to be paired with bay, basil, lemon balm, ginger, and bergamot in money, success, happiness, and manifestation spells. Citrine is one of the few crystals that can remove negative energy on its own, making it unnecessary to be continuously cleansed.

CLEAR QUARTZ

Clear quartz is a very universal crystal that can be used in all your tea witchery. It is a master healer and amplifies whatever energy is within your intentions. It absorbs, stores, reflects, amplifies, balances, and focuses energy. It lends a balancing effect on the emotions and promotes a healthy immune system. It aligns all the chakras, and therefore also balances your spellwork. But it especially represents the crown chakra. It may be used within your herbs, your water, teapot, and magick. It perfectly pairs with rosemary, peppermint, lemon, cinnamon, and cloves in protection, healing, and cleansing tea magick.

JASPER

The stone of protection. This crystal balances the energies—the yin/
yang—making it a good grounding stone. Promotes mental clarity and
focus. Calms the senses, allowing the receiver to relax and organize
their thoughts. It could possibly heal the productive system and
deliver strength and vitality. Jasper harmonizes the mind, body, and
soul, helping protect them from illness and diseases. Depending upon
the color of this stone, it will associate with a chakra point, but often
it is connected to the root and sacral chakras. May be used in your
herbs and held during ceremony. Loves to be paired with jasmine,
marjoram, nutmeg, orange, and mint in strength, luck, and protection
tea magick.

MOONSTONE

The stone of new beginnings. The crystals have always been deeply
associated with the energies of the moon and with moon deities.
Moonstone enhances the psychic abilities, intuition, clairvoyance, and
development of the psychic abilities. It is believed to heal conditions
connected to the reproductive system and hormones, especially for
conception, pregnancy, and childbirth. It soothes emotional and
spiritual imbalances and stress. May also be used to cleanse karmic
pain passed down generationally. It raises the vibrations of the third
eye, throat, and crown chakras. May be used in your herbs, water,
teapot, tea altar, and magick. Pairs wonderfully with jasmine, yarrow,
cinnamon, and mugwort in psychic work, dreams, protection,
courage, and manifestation tea magick.

ROSE QUARTZ

Rose quartz is the stone of gentleness, otherwise known as the stone of the heart. It inspires and promotes energies toward love and beauty and expands these vibrations to the self and the environment, as well as to the universe, making it the perfect crystal for petitions to the guiding spirits and deities. An ideal gem to have upon a tea altar dedicated to a god or goddess or the ancestors. It lends a powerful effect on the heart and emotions and is associated with the heart chakra, making this gem the best for soothing tempers, asking for forgiveness, and inspiring love and passion. It may be used with your herbs, your water, teapot, and magick. It gently pairs with rose, lavender, and violet blossoms in love, healing, forgiveness, and encouraging tea magick. It is best to cleanse this gem with water, and let it dry under the light of the moon.

SMOKY QUARTZ

The grounding stone. An excellent gem to combat negative emotions and protect the energies from stressful vibrations and nightmares. It brings clarity of mind and helps bring balance during meditations and psychic work. Ideal crystals to aid in magick where you want to change bad moods to good, or to banish negative feelings and replace them with positive ones. An ideal stone for protection and to prepare the body for astral projection during sleep. The crystal will always help bring a person back to reality. Protects against bad influences and negative materialistic affairs. Also a good crystal for business and finances. Brings grounding vibrations to the root chakra. May be used within your herbs, water, teapot, and magick. Pairs with rosemary, spearmint, basil, bergamot, and marigold in protection, grounding, money, and psychic tea magick.

TIGER'S EYE

The crystal of confidence. This gem inspires higher self-esteem and the ability to overcome inner struggles and life's difficulties by soothing and bringing emotional balance and clarity. It strengthens mental willpower and brings protection and luck. It motivates the bearer to go with the flow and overcome fears. Increases peace and relaxation. It is associated with the sacral and solar-plexus chakras. May be used within the tea, tea altar, and beside the teapot. Best when paired with lemon, orange, chamomile, peppermint, and bergamot in courage, clarity, luck, and protection tea magick.

Herbal Preparations

The tea witch's kitchen is the center of magickal life and healing. Although tea is the main conduit of magick for the tea witch, you must always consider the other ingredients that are involved to aid in empowering magickal work and healing. This chapter will present ingredients that can be directly mixed into your brews in order enhance the power of your tea spell and rituals. Ingredients like the sugar cane can lend their energy to sweeten any spell, and the life-giving essence of honey can help manifest any remedy. Milks of different varieties also give their powers to a spell. Then there is the beauty of ingredients that can transform your meals through the power of magickal herbal infused oils and salts. These all fall into the categories of herbal decoctions, electuaries, oils, and tinctures, and all of them can play a powerful role in your magick.

Decoctions

A decoction is for tough herb parts such as bark, roots, and heavy leaves simmered in water.

You'll need:

1 ounce of dried herbs
1 pint of water

Bring the water to a boil and mix in the dried herbs. Reduce heat and let the herbs simmer for around 30 minutes. The simmering time will vary and may even take up to an hour depending entirely on the herbs being used. Decoctions should then be strained while hot. Use glass, ceramic, or earthenware pots, or clean enameled cast iron. Do not use plain cast iron with astringent herbs since the iron will leach into your brew. Decoctions are ideal for harsher and more powerful spells and rituals.

Electuaries

An electuary is comprised of powders mixed with syrups, honey, or sugars to create a magickal or medicinal sweet and powerful tasting remedy to add to your spells or daily healthy life. These are prepared when needed. Different substances use different proportions of syrup. Lighter herbs and flowers require twice their weight, while gum resins need two thirds of their weight. But primarily:

1 ounce dry ingredients to 1 pint of sugary substance

Soak the dry and wet together and let sit for a day and a half. Then strain. Electuaries must be used quickly since over time, they will begin to harden. If honey or syrup is used and hardens, simply add more syrup/honey, or place in a mildly warm bowl of water to soften. Sugars may be mixed with herbal powders and then made into cubes or molds.

SUGGESTED SWEETENERS

Agave Syrup—Love. Lust. Hexing. Controlling. Courage.
    Strength. Healing.

Coconut Sugar—Purification. Protection. Lunar Magick.

Date Sugar—Spirituality. Transformation. Offerings. Love.

Honey—Binding, Attraction, Love.

Maple Syrup—Love. Spirituality. Healing. Psychic Powers.

Sugar—Love, Purification, Attraction.

ELECTUARY RECIPES FOR SPECIFIC USES

Banishing: Mix 2 parts black tea, 1 part angelica root, and 1
    part clove. Add to a jar and cover with agave syrup.

Healing: Mix equal parts of garlic, cinnamon, lemon balm, and
    mint. Fill a jar full and cover with honey.

Peaceful Home: Mix two parts rose petals with one part cumin. Add
    two tablespoons of this blend to two ounces of white sugar.

Protection: Mix 2 parts marigold petals, one part cinnamon,
    and one part clove. Add two tablespoons of this blend to
    two ounces of coconut sugar.

Psychic Power: Mix 2 parts rose petals, 12 threads of saffron,
    and one part star anise. Add to a jar and cover with maple
    syrup. Add a pinch of cinnamon.

Spirit Offering: Mix 2 parts rooibos, 1 part cinnamon, 1 part
    ginger. Add two tablespoons of this blend to two ounces of
    date sugar.

Aromatic Oils

Creating aromatic oils is a two-step process. In creating these oils, you are going to extract the essence of your magickal herbs into an oil, which can then be used in any number of ways: you can use them for cooking, to anoint magickal tools, to apply on the body, and so on.

Step one: To make an oil, pick out fresh or dried quality herbs. Pack a large jar with your chosen herb blend and then pour in a favorite monounsaturated or polyunsaturated oil. I prefer olive oil. Use enough oil to cover the herbs, then close the jar tightly, and place it in a sunny place for four weeks. Strain out the herb by pouring contents through a cheesecloth into a fresh jar. Be sure to squeeze the cheesecloth at the end in order to get all the oil out of the herbs before discarding. You now have your first batch of oil.

Step two: Now you will repeat the process a second time. Repack a clean jar with a fresh batch of the same herb blend. Cover it with the oil previously infused in step one (you may add a little of the original source oil if necessary in order to completely fill the jar and cover the herbs). Store again in sunlight, shaking every other day, for four weeks, then strain again through cheesecloth. Pour the oil into a labeled and dated jar and store until needed. Oils are helpful when an extra touch of power is needed for brews or when needed for extra control over a situation.

SUGGESTED OILS

Almond Oil—For Gentle Aid. Blessings. Multipurpose. Protection.
    Children Protection. Pure Love. Use within 9 months.

Avocado Oil—Love. Aphrodisiac. Procreation. Business. Money matters. Manifestation. Use within 3 months.

Grape-seed Oil—Spiritual development. Spiritual Love. The Spiritual Dimension. Use within 3 to 4 months.

Olive Oil—Money. Success. Manifestation. Rich Love. Prosperity. Good Health. Use within 9 months to a year.

Sunflower Oil—Superior Results. Growth. Sun Energy. Boost of Power. Prosperity. Fast Love. Lasts for a year.

OIL RECIPES FOR SPECIFIC USES

Blessing Oil: Mix two parts rosemary and one part bay. Add two tablespoons of this blend to two ounces of almond oil.

Courage Oil: Mix equal parts of rosemary, cinquefoil, thyme, and yarrow. Add two tablespoons of this blend to two ounces of sunflower oil. Sprinkle in a pinch of ginger.

Dream Oil: Mix equal parts of lemon peel, lemongrass, and mugwort. Use two tablespoons of this blend to two ounces of grape seed oil.

Love Oil: Mix equal parts of jasmine, rose petals, lavender, and cinnamon. Use two tablespoons of this blend in two ounces of avocado oil.

Luck Oil: Mix three parts cinnamon, one part orange peel, and one part star anise. Use two tablespoons of this blend to two ounces of olive oil. Sprinkle in a pinch of ginger and allspice.

Alcohol Tinctures

Tinctures are potion solutions of herbs in alcohol or diluted alcohol. To make a tincture, grind down herbs with a mortar and pestle or a blender. Add just enough high-quality vodka, whiskey, rum, gin, or grain alcohol to cover the herbs. Let it sit for three weeks. Then add two tablespoons of glycerin per pint of liquid, and about a 10 percent volume (roughly 3 tablespoons) of pure spring water.

Because liquid volumes can tricky, and because you're working with alcohol, below is a basic conversion chart. As you can see, following the above instructions, you will be using over half a bottle— around five-eighths—of your chosen alcohol.

One standard bottle of alcohol	25 oz	750 ml
One pint	16 oz	473 ml
10 percent of	16 oz	1.6 oz
One tablespoon		.5 oz

Strain and store your tincture in airtight amber-colored glass. If kept cool and out of direct sunlight, tinctures may last for up to five years. When you add to tea, the recommended dose is about 15 to 20 drops. If you wish to make your tea nonalcoholic, you can "burn off" or evaporate the alcohol in the following way: Add the tincture to your teacup, and then add ¼ teaspoon of boiling water.

Tinctures add a power punch to spells and are most ideal during sabbats and esbats. Below are some of my favorites, indicating their magickal use properties.

Everclear—Healing. Health.

Gin—Visions. Clarity. Mental Powers.

Rum—Love. Lust. Attraction. Persuasion.

Vodka—Grounding. Protection. Sympathetic Magick. Love. Lust.

Whiskey—Money. Protection.

Milk Tinctures

If you do not want to use an alcohol solution tincture, you may substitute milk for alcohol. Your herb blend will then create a milk tincture. You will prepare your herb blend in the same way, crushing in a mortar and pestle or blender. Using about 1 tablespoon of this prepared herb blend, add 1½ cups of milk of your choice; see the recommendations below. You may optionally add spices and/or a sweetener. Heat over medium heat until warmed through—do not boil! Then strain out the herbs and store in a labeled, dated jar in the refrigerator. Milk tinctures do not last long: you must keep in mind the expiration date of the type of milk you are using.

SUGGESTED MILKS

Almond Milk—Healing. Prosperity. Wealth. Wisdom.

Coconut Milk—Cleansing. Protection.

Milk/Cream—Nurturing. Power. Protection. Wishes.

Nut Milk (cashew, hazelnut, walnut, etc.)—Fertility. Love. Prosperity. Wishes.

Oat Milk—Grounding. Health. Prosperity.

Soy Milk—Protection. Luck. Success.

ADDITIONS TO MILK TINCTURES

Energy: Mix 2 parts peppermint, 1 part matcha tea, and 1 part ginger. Add blend to 2 cups of oat milk and bring to medium heat. Add agave syrup.

Purification: Mix 2 parts chamomile, lavender, and coconut pieces; 1 part black tea and 1 part ginger and turmeric. Add mix to 2 cups of milk and bring to medium heat. Add white sugar.

Self-love: Mix 2 parts rose petals and white tea, 1 part cocoa powder, 1 pod of cardamom, 1 cinnamon stick, and 1 vanilla bean. Add blend to 2 cups of any nut milk variety of your choice. Bring to medium heat. Add honey.

Wisdom: Mix 2 parts chamomile and peaches and 1 part sage and walnut. Add blend to 2 cups of almond milk and bring to medium heat. Add date sugar.

Aromatic Vinegars

Herbs may also be steeped in vinegars to create an aromatic vinegar that may be used in cooking, washes, liniments, and preventative or dispelling magick. Place herbs in a clean jar and cover with vinegar. Put a lid on the jar and let stand in a sunny place for 21 days. After 21 days, the vinegar solution is strained, and the process repeated with new herbs covered with vinegar from the previous step for another 21 days, then strained and labeled. Vinegars may last for years. White vinegar is a universal ingredient and may be used in most spells.

Herbal Moon Water

Herbal moon waters are made with herbs left to soak in pure spring water that is then left outside beneath the moonlight during a full moon; it is left outside all night and brought in before dawn. The water may then be strained and bottled, and then used in spells and rituals. Store in a cool dark place. It is important to label the bottle with the date and astrological sign the full moon occurred in. You may use this water in accordance with the type of moon water you wish to make, or use it to boil and infuse within your tea witchery. Each astrological sign will lend its own gifts and energy to the water and brew.

The Tea Magick Continues

In the end, the tea has been made, the spells have been cast, the rituals celebrated. And now the tea witch has a unique conundrum, one not found in other forms of magickal working. In other magickal practices, candles will burn down, incense will turn to smoke and dissipate, the tarot cards are put away. But tea witches are left with the remnants of their lovingly concocted teas. Perhaps you have already taken advantage of this moment to work tasseomancy, the divination technique of reading the tea leaves. Now what? Most tea witches are left with no idea what to do with the precious steeped herbs after the magick is said and done.

Most of the time, the used and usually wet tea blend is simply thrown away, with no consideration of the energy that still resides within. And there is so much more that could be done with your magickal brew instead of unceremoniously tossing it away! Is there still enchantment left in the leaves? The answer to that question is yes. After you've used your tea in a spell or remedy, there is magick still working within those leaves, and depending on the kind of spell you manifested, the way you dispose of tea remnants matters. Just as with any other spell ingredient, you must keep in mind the power and symbolism of what you've created, and make an informed choice about how you discard your leftover residue. Plus, it is a good way to be eco-conscious and reduce, reuse, and recycle. The beautiful and positive thing about tea is that it is highly reusable and biodegradable. This grimoire has been devoted to creating your own loose-leaf tea blends. Try to avoid purchasing teas that are sold in tea bags, as most bags contain small traces of plastic, making them not only a health hazard but also harmful to the environment. Alway use reusable tea bags made of cotton or use a tea strainer. Ultimately, all tea may be composted and fertilized within your magickal garden and be among other plants that harbor the same energies you manifested. Or your used tea remains may be taken outside the perimeter of your home, to add to the earth elsewhere. Never drop your tea down the sink, drain, garbage disposal, or toilet. That method of disposal will cause your spells to seriously backfire.

How you dispose of your tea remnants has magickal purpose. Let's look at different forms of disposal methods based on the intentions you blended and brewed the tea for initially.

TO ATTRACT

These remnants are for spell remedies that are cast to attract the energies of love, happiness, fortune, and abundance. Thus, they may be immediately watered or composted and used to fertilize plants by your front doorstep. They may be blended into the earth among plants like thyme, yarrow, catnip, apple tree, lemon balm, basil, chamomile, hibiscus, jasmine, peppermint, roses, rosemary, and tomato. The dried leaves may also be soaked in honey to release their energies and create a boosted sweetener to add to the foods or beverages you might serve to your intended. They can also be added to the foods being consumed by your ceremonial group in order continue your spell well after the tea party is over. The dried leaves are the perfect candidate for a soap additive.

TO BANISH

These remnants are for spell remedies that are used to banish—energies, people, or situations. The dried leaves may be thrown in a crossroads or burned by the back door and swept off the back doorstep. They may also be composted, fertilized, and buried in the ground far outside the perimeter of the home. Continue to use the tea's banishing vibrations by drying and heating them in an aroma lamp burner to banish influences within the home. Or, they may be soaked in vinegar and transformed into a cleaning agent to use around the home.

TO BIND

These remnants are for spell remedies used to bind spells, enemies, bad intentions, and so forth. They may be sealed in a small cotton bag and hidden in a cellar, closet, or a pot of dirt. They must be hidden in the dark, for no one to find, for only you yourself to know. The leaves may also be separately composted and fertilized over soil where potatoes are planted.

TO CLEANSE

These remnants are for spell remedies meant to cleanse a person, place, or situation. Depending on the intensity of the cleanse, the dried leaves may be burned and the ashes scattered outside. The dried leaves may also be placed in a cloth bag and hung in place around the home to continue absorbing the energy. They may be blended into candle wax to continue their purpose, or transformed into a cleaning agent to cleanse the home.

TO COMMUNICATE (WITH A SPIRIT OR DEITY)

These are remnants that are involved in spell remedies to communicate with the dead, with ancestors, guardians, or the gods. They may be dried and used as an offering, either by adding them to candle wax, anointing oils, or foods, or burned as an incense. The tea may also be used to soak eye patches and placed over the eyes to strengthen your connection with the spirits.

TO DESTROY

These remnants are for spell remedies purely intended to destroy hexes, spells cast against you, or enemies, or to exorcise entities. The remnants must be dried completely and then burned far away from your home. Or they may be soaked in vinegar and used as a spritz to continue destroying the negativity around you.

TO ENCOURAGE

These remnants are for spell remedies that were used for courage, mental vitality, psychic awareness, or influence. They may be composted, fertilized, and planted by the front doorstep, or placed in pots on a windowsill. They may be planted near thyme, grapes, rosemary, spearmint, lavender, violets, roses, marigolds, peppermint, and sage.

TO FIX

These remnants are for teas that have been used to soothe tempers, bring forgiveness, stop a couple from quarreling, and to mend a broken heart. The leaves may be dried and made into a tea pillow to be shared or kept among the intended. Or the remnants may be placed within a sachet to be hung or kept in the home. If the tea blend is nutritious, it may be incorporated in food recipes as well.

TO GLAMOUR

These remnants are for spell remedies that call for beauty and to convince others of your desired intentions. These teas may be left under a full moon over a mirror and, once dried, used to create face care products to continue their glamour magick.

TO HIDE

These tea remnants are for remedies held in secret—where the intended has no knowledge of the spell manifested, or when the brewer intends to be hidden from their enemies. This spell will never be spoken aloud by the brewer. The leaves may be placed in a small black cotton bag and buried within the property. The location must never be disclosed.

TO KEEP CLOSE

These tea remnants can be used for spell remedies you cast for items, energies, or people to remain close to you and close to home. Also used for protection. You may water, or compost, fertilize, and eventually bury these used brews in your backyard among plants like magnolias, lemon trees, lavenders, marjoram, tansies, and thyme. The tea remnants may also be dried and made into a tea pillow to sleep upon.

TO MOVE AWAY

These remnants are for spell remedies when you wish for the intended to part from you. They can be used for gentle banishing spells or used to dispel personal negativities, habits, and mental fog. The tea may be soaked once more overnight, in a teapot, and taken to a source of running water or an ocean. Let the moving waters carry these remnants away.

TO WISH

These remnants are for spell remedies that involve wishes and birthdays. The leaves may be dried and burned, then blown into the wind. Or they may be soaked in olive oil to release the magick inside and create a liquid seasoning for foods. They may also be dried and added to candle wax to continue their magick.

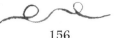

A Tea Witch's Words of Wisdom

The tea witch walks a sacred and ancient path. Within this grimoire, you've been gifted not only the wisdom of the ancestors, but also the wisdom of the earth. It is wise to connect with your chosen herbs through great empathy and visualization. You must use only a purified knife or clippers when harvesting. Before cutting, feel the herbs' energies, and offer a blessing.

Sacred herb, I ask thee to lend me your gifts and powers.
Aid me in my magickal life.
In return, I bless thee to grow stronger and more powerful than you once were.

Gently harvest what you need but never take more than is necessary. Do your research and always be sure you know how to harvest specific plants before cutting them. It is gracious to leave an offering before stepping away; this can be fertilizer, water, tea, milk, grain, crystals, cinnamon, copper pennies, and so forth.

And know…

When you choose to walk this path, it becomes your responsibility to understand both the benefits and effects the herbs do body. You become a keeper and a protector of your own health and the health of others. Be wise and aware of the balance, both physically and magickly.

Seek knowledge and continue to grow in your craft.

The Tea Witch's Rune

Larksome delight and radiant gloom.
Leaf to root, and trunk to limb.
Darken to the enchantress croon.
Here come thee to the hymn.

Ruler of Runes, Empress of Ash,
With Master of the dirt and the grass.
Bestow thy desire lightning flash,
Moil thy power onto this lass.

Within the force of wind and sand,
Within the spirit of star and seed,
As the spell is done, dance to the land.

A Tea Witch's Creed

Thou shall always respect the copper kettle,
For copper is a sacred metal that transforms magick into being.

•

Find a faithful friend in a cast-iron pot.
It will never fail in delivering its strength and power.

Trust in your herbs,
Raise them right, and they will stay with you till the end.

Do not trust in the fae,
To make you a good cup of tea.

A magickal teacup should be blessed by the elements,
Drowned in water, buried in soil, warmed over a candle,
or air dried on a windy day.

Ponder the meaning of full when you fill your kettle,
Then ponder the meaning of sacrifice when there is nothing left to pour.

Get lost at the bottom of a good brew,
But always find your way back to the light.

The moon loves to watch her garden be put to good use.
Harvest when she is full and can bless your efforts.

Herbs shall always be hung and dried from east to west,
To pay respects to the sun and moon for their aid.

Fire is a sweet-talking companion.
It must be flattered to get the best tasting tea.

When you are called, you must answer.
There are those that will always need your tea.

Tables and
Correspondences

Table of Brewing Times

These are the time limits and temperatures for brewing tea. This is based on one teaspoon of herbal blend per 8 ounces of water. All temperatures are Fahrenheit.

Instructions for the tea plant, *Camellia sinensis.*

WHITE TEA

Hot: 1.5 tsp—175 degrees—2 to 4 minutes

Cold: 3 tsp—175 degrees—2 to 4 minutes

GREEN TEA

Hot: 1 tsp—175 degrees—45 seconds to1 minute

Cold: 2 tsp—175 degrees—45 seconds to 1 minute

OOLONG TEA

Hot: 1 tsp—195 degrees—3 minutes

Cold: 2 tsp—195 degrees—3 minutes

BLACK TEA

  Hot: 1 tsp—195 to 205 degrees—2 to 3 minutes

  Cold: 2 tsp—195 to 205 degrees—2 to 3 minutes

• • •

For teas from the plant genus *Aspalathus linearis.*

ROOIBOS TEA

  Hot: 1.5 tsp—208 degrees—5 to 6 minutes

  Cold: 3 tsp—208 degrees—8 to 15 minutes

• • •

For all other plants.

HERBAL TEA

  Hot: 1.5 tsp—208 degrees—5 to 6 minutes

  Cold: 3 tsp—208 degrees—8 to 15 minutes

A Witch's Kitchen Conversion Table

For tea witches in lands near and far, and for those who work in different systems of weight and measurement, this handy table will help you convert measurements for ingredients. Keep in mind that tea making is an art, not a science. The measurements in this book for dry herbs will obviously vary from substance to substance. Milliliters generally measure liquid volume, whereas grams measure volume by weight. A tablespoon of dried leaves weighs less than a tablespoon of honey, for example. The differences can be slight, but as you perfect your recipes, determining quantities will become second nature to you. Generally if you're working in the metric system, use milliliters for liquids, and gram measurements for herbs.

MEASUREMENTS	TEMPERATURES

MEASUREMENTS

¼ tsp = 1.25 ml = 1 g

½ tsp = 2.5 ml = 2 g

1 tsp = 5 ml = 3.5 g

3 tsp = 1 tbsp

1 tbsp = 15 ml = 6.25 g

3 tbsp = 45 ml = 18.75 g

4 tbsp = ¼ cup = 60 ml

8 tbsp = ½ cup = 118 ml

A tad = ¼ tsp

A dash = ⅛ tsp

A pinch = 1/16 tsp

TEMPERATURES

F°	C°
175	80
	(alcohol boils)
200	94
212	100
	(water boils)
275	140
300	150
325	165
350	177
375	190
400	200
425	220

Magickal Goals and Intentions

ASTRAL PROJECTION

caraway

dandelion

fennel

hibiscus

marjoram

mugwort

parsley

BEAUTY

catnip

ginseng, American

CHASTITY

coconut

cucumber

hawthorn

lavender

pineapple

vervain

COURAGE

basil

borage

cohosh, black

ginger

mullein

nettle

pepper

rooibos

tea, black

thyme

yarrow

DIVINATION

cherry

dandelion

fig

goldenrod

hibiscus

lemongrass

marjoram

orange

pomegranate

tea, oolong

EXORCISM

angelica
basil
bergamot, orange
clove
clover
cumin
elder, American
garlic
horehound
juniper
lemon
lemongrass
lilac
mallow
mint
mullein
nettle
onion
peach
pepper
pine nut
rosemary
tea, black
thistle, milk
yarrow

FERTILITY

banana
carrot
cinnamon
coriander
cucumber
fig
geranium
grape
hawthorn
hazelnut
mint
mustard
nuts
palm, date
peach
pine nut
pomegranate
rice
tea, white

FIDELITY

chickweed
chili pepper
clover
cumin
elder, American

licorice

nutmeg

skullcap, American

yerba maté

FRIENDSHIPS

lemon

passionflower

tea, oolong

GOSSIP—TO HALT

clove

HAPPINESS

catnip

cinnamon

feverfew

hawthorn

lavender

marjoram

mint

saffron

tea, white

thyme

vanilla

HEALING—TO PROMOTE

allspice

almond

angelica

apple

balm, lemon

barley

bay

bergamot, orange

blackberry

chamomile

cinnamon

citron

cucumber

elder, American

fennel

garlic

ginseng, American

hemp

hops

horehound

lime

mint

mugwort

nettle

onion

pepper

peppermint

plum
potato
rose
rosemary
saffron
sorrel
spearmint
tea, green
thistle, milk
thyme
vervain
violet
willow

HEALTH—TO MAINTAIN
allspice
angelica
bergamot, orange
caraway
cinnamon
chamomile
coriander
galangal
geranium
juniper
marjoram
mullein

nutmeg
oats
sorrel
thyme
walnut

HEXES—TO BREAK
bergamot, orange
chili pepper
galangal
lemongrass
thistle, milk
vetiver

IMMORTALITY
apple
chrysanthemum
linden
sage
tea, green

LONGEVITY
lavender
lemon
maple
peach

sage
tea, green

LOVE
apple
apricot
bachelor's button
balm, lemon
barley
basil
Brazil nut
cardamom
catnip
chamomile
cherry
chestnut
chickweed
chili pepper
cinnamon
clove
clover
cohosh, black
coriander
damiana
dill
elecampane
fig

geranium
ginger
ginseng, American
hemp
hibiscus
jasmine
juniper
lavender
lemon
lemon verbena
licorice
lime
linden
lovage
mallow
maple
marjoram
nuts
orange
papaya
peach
pear
peppermint
plum
raspberry
rose
rosemary
saffron

skullcap, American
spearmint
strawberry
sugarcane
tea
thyme
tormentil
valerian
vanilla
vervain
vetiver
violet
willow
wormwood
yarrow
yerba maté

LOVE DIVINATION
mullein
rose
willow

LOVE SPELLS—TO BREAK
pistachio

LUCK
allspice
almond
chamomile
hazelnut
honeysuckle
linden
nutmeg
orange
pineapple
pomegranate
rose
star anise
strawberry
vanilla
vetiver
violet

LUST—TO DECREASE
vervain

LUST—TO INCREASE
caraway
cardamom
carrot
celery
cinnamon

damiana
dill
galangal
garlic
ginger
ginseng, American
hibiscus
lemongrass
licorice
lemon leaf
mint
nettle
onion
parsley
rosemary
saffron
tea, green
vanilla
violet
yerba maté

MENTAL POWERS—TO STRENGTHEN

caraway
celery
ginger
grape

horehound
lemongrass
marjoram
orange
peppermint
rooibos
rosemary
savory, summer
spearmint
tea
walnut

MONEY

allspice
almond
basil
bergamot, orange
blackberry
buckwheat
cashew
chamomile
cinnamon
cinquefoil
clove
clover
dill
elder, American

fenugreek

galangal

ginger

goldenrod

grape

honeysuckle

jasmine

maple

marjoram

mint

nutmeg

oats

onion

orange

pecan

pineapple

pomegranate

rice

spearmint

tea, black

vanilla

vervain

vetiver

woodruff

PEACE

balm, lemon

lavender

marjoram

mint

passionflower

sage

skullcap, American

thyme

vervain

violet

POWER

ginger

lemongrass

tea

PROPHETIC DREAMS

cinquefoil

dandelion

hibiscus

jasmine

lemongrass

marigold

mugwort

onion

rose

PROSPERITY

almond
banana
chamomile
cinnamon
ginger
honeysuckle
nuts
oats
vanilla

PROTECTION

agrimony
angelica
anise
barley
basil
bay
bergamot, orange
blackberry
blueberry
caraway
chrysanthemum
cinnamon
cinquefoil
clove
clover
coconut
cohosh, black
cumin
dill
elder, American
elecampane
fennel
galangal
garlic
geranium
ginseng, American
hazelnut
honeysuckle
horehound
hyssop
juniper
lavender
lilac
lime
linden
mallow
marigold
marjoram
mint
mugwort
mullein
nettle
onion

papaya
parsley
pepper
peppermint
plum
raspberry
rice
rose
rosemary
sage
tea, white
thistle, milk
tormentil
valerian
vervain
violet
willow
woodruff
wormwood

PSYCHIC POWERS
acacia
bay
borage
celery
cinnamon
citron

elecampane
galangal
honeysuckle
lemongrass
marigold
marjoram
mugwort
orange
peppermint
rose
saffron
star anise
thyme
wormwood
yarrow

PURIFICATION
acacia
anise
bay
chamomile
coconut
fennel
hyssop
lavender
lemon
lemongrass

lemon verbena
parsley
peppermint
rosemary
sugarcane
tea
thistle, milk
thyme
turmeric
valerian
vervain

SLEEP

agrimony
chamomile
cinquefoil
elder, American
hops
lavender
linden
passionflower
peppermint
rosemary
thyme
valerian
vervain

SPIRITS—TO CALL

dandelion
tea, pu-erh
thistle, milk
wormwood

SPIRITUALITY

acacia
cinnamon
ginger
tea

STRENGTH

bay
mugwort
rooibos
saffron
tea, black
thistle, milk

SUCCESS

almond
balm, lemon
bay
chamomile
cinnamon

clover
ginger
honeysuckle
marjoram
rosemary
saffron
vanilla

VISIONS
angelica
damiana
lemongrass

WISDOM
almond
chamomile
dill
ginger
peach
peppermint
rooibos
sage
tea

WISHES
dandelion
ginseng, American
hazelnut
pomegranate
sage
violet
walnut

YOUTH—TO MAINTAIN
anise
rosemary
vervain

Herbs by Elemental Attribute

The four elements—Earth, Air, Fire, Water—are traditionally associated with either feminine or masculine energy. These designations go back thousands of years. When working with these energies it's important to keep in mind that "masculine" and "feminine" are not the same as "male" and "female." These energetic designations have nothing to do with gender or sexual identity. In other traditions, these complementing energies are labeled in many other ways, such as yin/yang, above/below, action/intuition, and so forth. When working with herbs for elemental magick, you are working with these masculine and feminine energetic qualities—these are not herbs for males or herbs for females.

EARTH

Feminine energy. These herbs are best used in magicks for:

MONEY. PROSPERITY. FERTILITY. HEALING. EMPLOYMENT. PROTECTION. NATURE. GROUNDING. STRENGTH. SUCCESS. STABILITY. WISDOM. DEATH. REBIRTH. TRUTH. ABUNDANCE.

barley	horehound	sorrel
buckwheat	mugwort	vervain
honeysuckle	oats	vetiver

AIR

Masculine energy. These herbs are best used in magicks for:

MENTAL POWERS. VISIONS. PSYCHIC POWERS. WISDOM. ASTRAL
PROJECTION. THOUGHTS. CLARITY. KNOWLEDGE. DIVINATION.
MEMORY. SHADOW WORK. VISUALIZATION. CREATIVITY. NEW
BEGINNINGS. PURIFICATION. INSPIRATION.

acacia	dandelion	mint
agrimony	elecampane	palm, date
almond	fenugreek	parsley
anise	goldenrod	pecan
bergamot, orange	hazelnut	pine
borage	lavender	pistachio
Brazil nut	lemongrass	rice
caraway	lemon verbena	sage
chicory	linden	savory, summer
citron	maple	star anise
clover	marjoram	

FIRE

Masculine energy. These herbs are best used in magicks for:

LUST. COURAGE. STRENGTH. EXORCISM. PROTECTION. HEALTH.
PURIFICATION. HEALING. ENERGY. DESTRUCTION. POWER.
WILLPOWER. SEXUALITY. PASSION. TRANSFORMATION.

allspice
angelica
basil
bay
calendula
carrot
cashew
celery
chestnut
chili pepper
chrysanthemum
cinnamon
cinquefoil
clove
cumin
damiana
dill

fennel
fig
galangal
garlic
ginger
ginseng
hawthorn
hyssop
lime
marigold
mullein
mustard
nettle
nutmeg
olive
onion
orange

pepper
peppermint
pineapple
pomegranate
rooibos
rosemary
saffron
tangerine
tea
thistle, milk
tormentil
walnut
woodruff
wormwood
yerba maté

WATER

Feminine energy. These herbs are best used in magicks for:

SLEEP. MEDITATION. PURIFICATION. PROPHETIC DREAMS. HEALING. LOVE. FRIENDSHIPS. FIDELITY. ILLUSIONS. ENCHANTMENTS. DIVINATION. DREAMS. EMOTIONS. INTUITION. LUNAR MAGICK. REFLECTION. PEACE.

apple
apricot
aster
bachelor's button
balm, lemon
banana
blackberry
cardamom
catnip
chamomile
cherry
chickweed
coconut
cucumber
elder

feverfew
geranium
grape
hemp
hibiscus
jasmine
lemon
licorice
lilac
lily
mallow
papaya
passionflower
peach
pear

plum
raspberry
rose
skullcap
spearmint
strawberry
sugarcane
thyme
valerian
vanilla
violet
willow
yarrow

Herb Substitutions

Depending on your geographic location and the time of year, you may find that certain herbs are not available in your area. If necessary, the following substitutions are recommended.

Bergamot—Half lemon peel/half orange peel

Chamomile—Jasmine

Cinnamon—Nutmeg, or any spice

Clove—Nutmeg

Dandelion—May substitute any roots or toxic plants

Ginger—Cinnamon

Hemp—Bay

Hyssop—Lavender

Jasmine—Rose Petals

Juniper Berries—Pine

Lavender—Rose Petals

Lemon—May substitute any fruits

Lemongrass—Lemon Peel

Lemon Peel—Lemongrass

Lemon Verbena—Lemongrass

Marigolds—Rose Petals

Mint—Sage

Mugwort—Dandelion Leaf

Nutmeg—Cinnamon

Orange Peel—Tangerine Peel

Peppermint—Spearmint

Pine—Juniper berries

Rose—Yarrow

Rosemary—Thyme, or any herb

Rose Petals—May substitute any flowers

Saffron—Orange Peel

Sage—Mints

Spearmint—Peppermint

Tea—Rooibos

Thyme—Rosemary

Vanilla—Woodruff

Woodruff—Vanilla Bean

Wormwood—Dandelion Leaf

Yarrow—Rose Petals

Herbs by Latin Name

ACACIA—*Acacia senegal*

AGRIMONY—*Agrimonia eupatoria*

ALFALFA—*Medicago sativa*

ALLSPICE—*Pimenta officinalis or P. dioica*

ALMOND—*Prunus dulcis*

ANGELICA—*Angelica archangelica*

ANISE—*Pimpinella anisum*

APPLE—*Pyrus spp.*

APRICOT—*Prunus armeniaca*

ASTER—*Callistephus chinensis*

BACHELOR'S BUTTON—*Centaurea cyanus*

BALM, LEMON—*Melissa officinalis*

BANANA—*Musa sapientum*

BARLEY—*Hordeum vulgare*

BASIL—*Ocimum basilicum*

BAY—*Laurus nobilis*

BERGAMOT, ORANGE—*Mentha citrata*

BLACKBERRY—*Rubus villosus*

BLUEBERRY—*Vaccinium sect. Cyanococcus*

BORAGE—*Borago officinalis*

BRAZIL NUT—*Bertholletia excelsa*

BUCKWHEAT—*Fagopyrum spp.*

CARAWAY—*Carum carvi*

CARDAMOM—*Elettaria cardamomum*

CARNATION—*Dianthus caryophyllus*

CARROT—*Daucus carota*

CASHEW—*Anacardium occidentale*

CATNIP—*Nepeta cataria*

CELERY—*Apium graveolens*

CHAMOMILE, ROMAN—*Chamaemelum nobile*

CHERRY—*Prunus avium*

CHESTNUT—*Castanea sativa*

CHICKWEED—*Stellaria media*

CHICORY—*Cichorium intybus*

CHILI PEPPER—*Capsicum spp.*

CHRYSANTHEMUM—*Chrysanthemum*

CINNAMON—*Cinnamomum verum*

CINQUEFOIL—*Potentilla*

CITRON—*Citrus medica*

CLOVE—*Syzygium aromaticum*

CLOVER—*Trifolium spp.*

COCONUT—*Cocos nucifera*

COHOSH, BLACK—*Cimicifuga racemosa*

CORIANDER—*Coriandrum sativum*

CUCUMBER—*Cucumis sativus*

CUMIN—*Cuminum cyinum*

DAMIANA—*Turnera diffusa*

DANDELION—*Taraxacum officinale*

DILL—*Anethum graveolens*

ECHINACEA—*Echinacea angustifolia*

ELDER, AMERICAN—*Sambucus canadensis*

ELECAMPANE—*Inula helenium*

FENNEL—*Foeniculum vulgare*

FENUGREEK—*Trigonella foenum-graecum*

FEVERFEW—*Tanacetum parthenium*

FIG—*Ficus carica*

GALANGAL—*Alpinia galanga*

GARLIC—*Allium sativum*

GERANIUM—*Pelargonium*

GINGER—*Zingiber officinale*

GINSENG, AMERICAN—*Panax quinquefolius*

GOLDENROD—*Solidago*

GRAPE—*Vitis vinifera*

HAWTHORN—*Crataegus oxyacantha*

HAZELNUT, AMERICAN—*Corylus americana*

HEMP—*Cannabis sativa*

HIBISCUS—*Hibiscus spp.*

HONEYSUCKLE—*Lonicera*

HOPS—*Humulus lupulus*

HYSSOP—*Hyssopus officinalis*

JASMINE—*Jasminum officinale*

LAVENDER—*Lavandula officinalis*

LEMON—*Citrus limon*

LEMONGRASS—*Cymbopogon citratus*

LEMON VERBENA—*Lippia citriodora*

LETTUCE—*Lactuca sativa*

LICORICE—*Glycyrrhiza glabra*

LILAC—*Syringa vulgaris*

LILY—*Lilium brownii*

LIME—*Citrus x aurantiifolia*

LINDEN—*Tilia xeuropaea*

MALLOW—*Malva sylvestris*

MAPLE—*Acer spp.*

MARIGOLD—*Calendula officinalis*

MARJORAM—*Origanum majorana*

MINT—*Mentha spp.*

MUGWORT—*Artemisia vulgaris*

MULLEIN—*Verbascum thapsus*

MUSTARD SEED—*Sinapis alba*

NETTLE—*Urtica dioica*

NUTMEG—*Myristica fragrans*

OATS—*Avena sativa*

OLIVE—*Olea europaea*

ONION—*Allium cepa*

ORANGE—*Citrus sinensis*

PALM, DATE—*Phoenix dactylifera*

PANSY—*Viola tricolor*

PAPAYA—*Carica papaya*

PARSLEY—*Petroselinum crispum*

PASSIONFLOWER—*Passiflora incarnata*

PEACH—*Prunus persica*

PEAR—*Pyrus communis*

PECAN—*Carya illinoinensis*

PEPPER—*Piper nigrum*

PEPPERMINT—*Mentha piperita*

PINE—*Pinus spp.*

PINEAPPLE—*Ananas comosus*

PISTACHIO—*Pistacia vera*

PLUM—*Prunus domestica*

POMEGRANATE—*Punica granatum*

POTATO—*Solanium tuberosum*

RASPBERRY—*Rubus idaeus*

RICE—*Oryza sativa*

ROOIBOS—*Aspalathus linearis*

ROSE—*Rosa spp.*

ROSEMARY—*Rosmarinus officinalis*

SAFFRON—*Crocus sativus*

SAGE—*Salvia officinalis*

SAVORY, SUMMER—*Satureja hortensis*

SKULLCAP, BLUE—*Scutellaria lateriflora*

SORREL—*Rumex acetosa*

SPEARMINT—*Mentha spicata*

STAR ANISE—*Illicium verum*

STRAWBERRY—*Fragaria vesca*

SUGARCANE—*Saccharum officinarum*

TEA—*Camellia sinensis*

THISTLE, MILK—*Silybum marianum*

THYME—*Thymus vulgaris*

TORMENTIL—*Potentilla erecta*

TURMERIC—*Curcuma longa*

VALERIAN—*Valeriana officinalis*

VANILLA—*Vanilla aromatica*

VERVAIN—*Verbena officinalis*

VETIVER—*Chrysopogon zizanioides*

VIOLET—*Viola odorata*

WALNUT—*Juglans regia*

WILLOW—*Salix alba*

WOODRUFF—*Asperula odorata*

WORMWOOD—*Artemisia absinthium*

YARROW—*Achillea millefolium*

YERBA MATÉ—*Ilex paraguariensis*

Index of Spells, Recipes, and Rituals

Sources

Baker, Margaret. *Gardener's Magic and Folklore Unbound.* New York: Universe Books, a division of Rizzoli International Publications, 1978.

Blackwell, Will H. *Poisonous and Medicinal Plants.* Hoboken NJ: Prentice Hall, 1989).

Blunt, Wilfrid and Sandra Raphael. *Illustrated Herbal.* London: Frances Lincoln, LTD., a division of Quarto Group, 1979.

Boland, Bridget. *Gardener's Magic and Other Old Wives' Lore.* London: Michael Omara Books, 2003.

Chevallier, Andrew. *Encyclopedia of Herbal Medicine: 550 Herbs and Remedies for Common Ailments.* London: DK, a division of Penguin Books, 2016.

Cunningham, Scott. *Cunningham's Encyclopedia of Crystal, Gem & Metal Magic.* Woodbury, MN: Llewellyn Publications, 1998.

———. *Cunningham's Encyclopedia of Magical Herbs.* MN: Llewellyn Publications, 1985.

———. *Divination for Beginners: Reading the Past, Present & Future.* Woodbury, MN: Llewellyn Publications, 2003.

Desantis, Lawrence, CHC, ND. *Herbology.* Algonquin IL: New Eden School of Natural Health & Herbal Studies (ND).

———. *Natural Health and Nutrition.* Algonquin IL: New Eden School of Natural Health & Herbal Studies (ND).

The Encyclopedia of Crystals, Herbs, and New Age Elements: An A to Z Guide to New Age Elements and How to Use Them. New York: Adams Media, 2016.

Hall, Judy. *The Crystal Bible*. Iola, WI: Krause Publications, 2003.

Jacob, Dorothy. *A Witch's Guide to Gardening*. Taplinger Publishing Company, 1965 (no longer in business).

Johnston, Sarah Iles. *Ancient Greek Divination*. New York: John Wiley, 2008.

Mégemont, Florence. *The Metaphysical Book of Gems and Crystals*. Rochester VT: Healing Arts Press, an imprint of Inner Traditions, 2007.

About the Author

S. M. Harlow discovered her love of the wildcraft over two decades ago, when, as a young girl, she found contentment among the trees and the wind. She found great peace and connection with herbs and how they brought magick into the everyday mundane world. Tea was a gift taught to her by a master, who showed her how spirituality and healing is found within its brewed depths. Harlow hopes to give the world the same passion and inspiration that was so humbly bestowed upon her.

When she is not writing, Harlow is studying to become a doctor of traditional naturopathy. She lives with her husband and son on their homestead in Alabama. This is her first book.

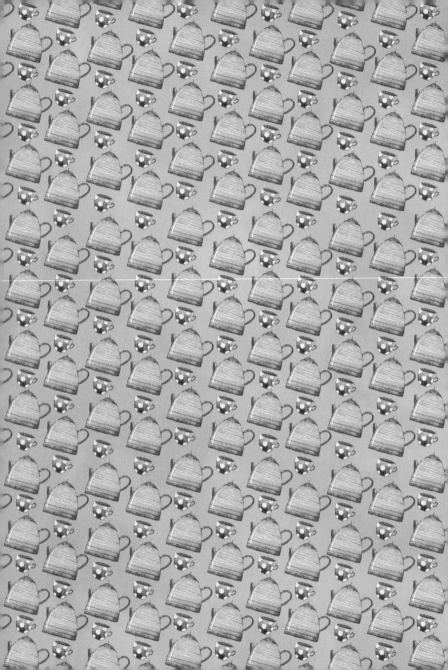